D1496328

UNDERSTANDING
HAROLD PINTER

Understanding Contemporary British Literature
Matthew J. Bruccoli, General Editor

volumes on

Kingsley Amis
John Fowles
Graham Greene
Doris Lessing
Iris Murdoch
Harold Pinter
Arnold Wesker
Paul West

UNDERSTANDING
Harold
PINTER

by RONALD KNOWLES

UNIVERSITY OF SOUTH CAROLINA PRESS

© 1995 by the University of South Carolina

Published in Columbia, South Carolina by the
University of South Carolina Press

Manufactured in the United States of America

99 98 97 96 95   5 4 3 2 1

Library of Congress Cataloging-in-Publication Data

Knowles, Ronald, 1940–
  Understanding Harold Pinter / by Ronald Knowles.
    p.   cm. —(Understanding contemporary British literature)
  Includes bibliographical references and index.
  ISBN 1–57003–044–8
  1. Pinter, Harold, 1930– —Criticism and interpretation.
I. Title. II. Series.
PR6066.I53Z714 1995
822'.914—dc20   95–4338

To Neil and Maggie
For friendship, hospitality, and Mozart

CONTENTS

EDITOR'S PREFACE

The volumes of *Understanding Contemporary British Literature* have been planned as guides or companions for students as well as good nonacademic readers. The editor and publisher perceive a need for these volumes because much of the influential contemporary literature makes special demands. Uninitiated readers encounter difficulty in approaching works that depart from the traditional forms and techniques of prose and poetry. Literature relies on conventions, but the conventions keep evolving; new writers form their own conventions, which in time may become familiar. Put simply, this book provides instruction in how to read certain contemporary writers—identifying and explicating their material, themes, use of language, point of view, structures, symbolism, and responses to experience.

The word *understanding* in the titles of books in this series was deliberately chosen. Many willing readers lack an adequate understanding of how contemporary literature works—that is, what the author is attempting to express and the means by which it is conveyed. Although the criticism and analysis in the series have been aimed at a level of general accessibility, these introductory volumes are meant to be applied in conjunction with the works they cover. They do not provide a substitute for the works and authors they introduce but, rather, prepare the reader for more profitable literary experiences.

M. J. B.

SOURCES AND ACKNOWLEDGMENTS

References in the text are to the following publications of Harold Pinter:

Plays One (London: Faber, 1991): *The Birthday Party, The Room, The Dumb Waiter, A Slight Ache, The Hothouse, A Night Out.*

Plays Two (London: Faber, 1991): *The Caretaker, Night School, The Dwarfs, The Collection, The Lover,* the revue sketches.

Plays Three (London: Faber, 1991): *The Homecoming, Tea Party, The Basement, Landscape, Silence,* "Night."

Plays Four (London: Faber, 1991): *Old Times, No Man's Land, Betrayal, One for the Road, Mountain Language, A Kind of Alaska, Victoria Station, Family Voices.*

"Precisely," *Harper's Magazine,* May 1985, 37.

Party Time (London: Faber, 1991).

Moonlight (London: Faber, 1993).

Five Screenplays (London: Eyre Methuen, 1971): *The Servant, The Pumpkin Eater, The Quiller Memorandum, Accident, The Go-Between.*

The French Lieutenant's Woman and Other Screenplays (London: Methuen, 1981): *The Last Tycoon, Langrishe, Go Down.*

The Heat of the Day (London: Faber, 1989).

The Comfort of Strangers and Other Screenplays (London: Faber, 1990): *Reunion, Turtle Diary, Victory.*

The Dwarfs (London: Faber, 1990).

"New World Order," *The Pinter Review: Annual Essays* (1991): 1–3.

Collected Poems and Prose (London: Faber, 1991).

Ten Early Poems (Warwick: Greville Press, 1992).

The Trial (London: Faber, 1993).

SOURCES AND ACKNOWLEDGMENTS

Harold Pinter's works are published in the United States by the Grove Press, New York.

A system of accurate quotation of Pinter's dialogue differentiating between his own ellipses and the conventions of critical publication would be distracting; therefore, a standard practice is adopted here to facilitate reading.

Harold Pinter is thanked for his generosity in answering queries, for supplying information, and for permission to reproduce the dust jacket photograph. Cheryl Foote is thanked for her word-processing professionalism, patience, and promptness. A version of comments on *The Heat of the Day* and much of the detail in chapter 8 first appeared in *The Pinter Review,* the editors of which are thanked for permission to publish here.

UNDERSTANDING
HAROLD PINTER

CHAPTER ONE

Career and Overview

Career

Harold Pinter is commonly considered the greatest English dramatist of his time, and in world terms he stands alongside the leading playwrights of the twentieth century. Over a period of more than thirty-five years Pinter's oeuvre amounts to over forty pieces for stage, screen, television, and radio which have been internationally translated and produced. It would take pages to list the honors, awards, prizes, and degrees conferred, throughout his career, at home and abroad. Yet there have always been those who have had difficulty in understanding, or have lacked sympathy for, Pinter's writing. It is hoped that this study will offer a helpful reappraisal by reconsidering the plays for all readers. First, the following "overview" section will largely use Pinter's own comments on his art as a foundation. In the generally chronological survey that follows, interpretation of the work will develop from the formulations of the early critical reception and will occasionally apply the particular critical insights offered by the rise of modern literary theory.

Born in 1930, Pinter was the only child of Hyman (Jack) Pinter, a ladies' tailor, and Frances (née Mann). Jack Pinter worked grueling hours to support his family, in their Victorian terrace house in the then respectable working-class district of Hackney in London's East End, as part of a close extended family within the Jewish community. Pinter's forebears originally came from Portugal via Hungary, like many such immigrants, to escape prejudice and pogroms and to find a better life. Like most Jewish boys, Pinter eventually did his bar mitzvah, though out of a sense of duty, rather than religious conviction. Yiddish was spoken in the home, and many years later Pinter characterized the vibrancy of the surrounding milieu as a "living community" with a "living language."[1] From this period Pinter's view of life has been secular; for him religious orthodoxy "was not fruitful: it wasn't positive because it was embattled, defensive, and protective."[2] To Pinter the label "working-class Jew" would be empty and misleading, indicating an ethnic and social generality worlds away from the realities of human experience he would eventually dramatize, in contrast to his contemporary Arnold Wesker, whose early work identified with the antifascist struggles of that community. Pinter has always felt a moral need, however, to bear witness to the Holocaust and to those, like Paul Celan and Primo Levi, whose testimony remains in literature.[3]

The young Pinter won a scholarship to Hackney Downs Grammar School, where he excelled both as an all-round athlete specializing in cricket and as an actor. The senior English master, Joseph Brearley, encouraged Pinter's love of literature and acting, and a debt of gratitude and affection was to remain with the dramatist, eventually finding oblique but powerful expression in a commemorative poem of 1987.[4] Of equal importance was the social aspect of these years. Pinter formed close and lasting bonds of friendship with both Jewish and non-Jewish peers in a harmonious atmosphere free from anti-Semitism. This was not the case at large in the East End of London, where Sir Oswald Mosley's Blackshirt Fascist panaceas included rabble-rousing anti-Semitism. At this stage can be seen the early contrasts that were to effect an acute sensitivity such as Pinter's profoundly— familial love, physical competition, friendship, physical threat, social hatred.

With the onset of war Pinter was evacuated to the relatively pastoral setting of Cornwall. Eventually, on his return, the Little Blitz of 1944 was to offer an altogether more fearful maturity than the contemporaneous bar mitzvah: Pinter recorded that "there were times when I would open our back door and find our garden in flames": "Our house never burned, but we had to evacuate several times. Every time we evacuated, I took my cricket bat with me."[5]

Pinter came to maturity in the postwar world of bomb-scarred London, the world of cold war peace. How could people reconcile the reality of peace—the resumption of the pedestrian, everyday world—with the reality of war and the Holocaust? The reappearance of Mosley's thugs in Pinter's neighborhood were a frightening reminder of the bureaucracy of genocide, the abduction from domestic hearth to gas chamber. Reacting with disgust and skepticism to that cold war situation, the eighteen-year-old Pinter was tried twice and fined as a conscientious objector on, it should be emphasized, political not pacifist grounds. Nightmare had become a reality from which the human imagination had to be relieved by "normality." Postwar music hall and films provided the rescue of laughter and romance, musicals, variety shows, and idealized war films. But something like the contemporary paintings of Francis Bacon—

Pinter was an early admirer—gave expression to that silent scream beneath the surface. As a potential condition of repressed hysteria, nightmare vied with normality, while the knowledge of what human beings are capable of doing to one another, and incapable of preventing, carried inescapable complicities of guilt. These feelings undergo an artistic transmutation and are eventually rediscovered as part of the experience of seeing, for example, *The Birthday Party* (1958).[6]

As a student at the Royal Academy of Dramatic Art, Pinter felt estranged by the middle-class assurance of his contemporaries, faked a nervous breakdown, and left to wander around London in what he nevertheless described as a "fruitful" period: writing poems, watching cricket, falling in love, and always listening and observing. After a few parts in radio drama Pinter joined Anew McMaster's repertory company and toured Ireland. At this juncture Pinter earned his living as an actor but aspired to be a poet and novelist, completing a highly stylized fiction, *The Dwarfs* (1990). Behind the aesthete was a world of contrasting experiences: domestic harmony and external threat; the amorphous sprawl of London yet a close-knit extended family; arguably the greatest atrocity in history and the routine habit of daily life. Seemingly turning away from all this, Pinter was transforming himself into a characteristic poet of the period. One of his close old school friends, Henry Woolf, then studying drama at Bristol University, asked for a short one-act play for a student production, thus providing the impetus for *The Room* (1957). The language of ordinary people saved Pinter from the ivory tower of postwar aestheticism. Pinter had found his métier.

In retrospect, the playwright's voluminous output falls into two main patterns. First, from approximately 1957 to 1963, the overwhelming power of that group of plays often referred to as "comedies of menace," or "theater of the absurd," including *The Birthday Party* (1958) and *The Caretaker* (1960); second were the "memory plays," from *Landscape* (1968) and *Silence* (1969) to *No Man's Land* (1975). Pinter's early contribution to British cinema, with Joseph Losey, may be divided by placing *The Servant* (1963) with the first group and *The Go-Between* (1971) with the second. Standing between is *The Homecoming* of 1965, arguably Pinter's most substantial and complex achievement. After *Betrayal* (1978), the title of which made explicit a lifelong concern of the dramatist, Pinter concentrated on film work, most famously with *The French Lieutenant's Woman* (1981). In the 1980s the political plays *One for the Road* (1984), *Mountain Language* (1988), and *Party Time* (1991) derived from Pinter's moral and political stand against the abuse of human rights, particularly in South America and Turkey and, indeed, in the United Kingdom. In recent years, flourishing in every way, as actor, artist, and director, Pinter has written the screenplay for Kafka's *Trial* (1993) and, the first since 1978, a full-length play, *Moonlight* (1993).

In 1956 Pinter married the actress Vivien Merchant, and a son, Daniel, was born in 1958. After divorce, Pinter married the historian and mystery writer Lady Antonia Fraser in 1980.

Overview

For purposes of an overview, a very useful approach is to examine Pinter's own response—in essays, lectures, and interviews—to the success, not to say notoriety, of his work, in reaction to media attention, professional criticism, and journalists' reviews. Pinter never thinks in abstract or theoretical terms about the nature of his writing. In fact, he never even makes a synopsis of a play.

After touring with Anew McMaster in Ireland, Pinter returned to London and joined Donald Wolfit's company (so brilliantly evoked in Ronald Harwood's play *The Dresser* [1980]), playing in Shakespeare. Thereafter, in the course of the 1950s, Pinter joined various repertory companies up and down the country acting in standard comedy, farce, and thriller. Pinter thinks intuitively, as an actor, and, as will be shown, the genesis of a Pinter play is more akin to the subconscious gestation of poetry than to the conscious ordering of scene and act, entrance and exit.

An indirect anticipation of a major impulse underlying Pinter's art was expressed in a letter of 1954 appraising the work of Samuel Beckett. On a tour in Ireland in 1949 Pinter came across an issue of *Irish Writing* which contained Beckett's "An Extract from *Watt*." This led the young actor-poet to immerse himself in the Irishman's prose, finding there some indefinable echo of his own inchoate stirrings, as he had found already in the writings of Kafka, which inspired his early prose pieces "Kullus" (1949) and "The Examination" (1955). In many respects these small works are prototypes of one of Pinter's principal concerns: possession and dispossession of place and person. After the success of *The Caretaker* Pinter met Beckett in Paris, and they became friends. Pinter subsequently sent him manuscript copies of his work. On opening a Beckett exhibition at the University of Reading in 1970, Pinter declared the author of *Waiting for Godot* to be "the greatest writer of our time"[7]—a view that remained, undiminished. In the 1954 letter Pinter writes: "I don't want philosophies, tracts, dogmas, creeds, way outs, truths, answers, *nothing from the bargain basement. He is the most courageous, remorseless writer going. . . . he hasn't got his hand over his heart.*"[8] Several things are implied here which were to be characteristics of Pinter's own writing. The artist as some kind of Olympian being of superior imagination and learning in possession of a visionary truth is rejected. The appeal to sentimentality and the voice of true feeling is denied. Sentimentality colored much of nineteenth-century culture and persisted in the twentieth century, particularly in social conditions of unemployment, depression, war, and its aftermath. People often need escapism, and for this to work properly it must reciprocally modify reality. Conscious use of entertainment for escapist relief is one thing; accepting the emollient gloss of escapism as reality is quite another. Antisentimentalism as almost a principle of Pinter's oeuvre is perhaps felt most strongly in *The Homecoming* and arose in an interview with Mel Gussow in 1971. Pinter denied the charge of coldness, even malice, in his portrayal of character and continued with this recognition: "I've always been concerned with trying to see them as clearly as possible, and without obviously a kind of falsity which is sentimentality. . . . It's so easy to sentimentalize yourself and characters and every damn thing really. . . . I feel now that I possibly have the capacity within me to, I hope, remain rigorous and unsentimental, true to what is actually taking place in these people, but not quite so tough."[9]

The phrase "taking place" is crucial for Pinter's drama and recurs elsewhere. Another related phrase that came up repeatedly in early interviews was "the living moment." Together they encapsulate the essential modality of Pinter's drama. The social nature of the theater itself reproduces these factors, since it fundamentally confronts the disjunction between groups of people: the audience observing what is "taking place," the characters experiencing "the living moment." This situation reflects that of life, in which most of the time there is no direct access into other peoples' minds and hearts and often only an unreliable view of our own experience. "When the curtain goes up on one of my plays, you're faced with a situation, a particular situation, two people sitting in a room, which hasn't happened before, and is just happening at this moment and we know no more about them than I know about you sitting at this table."[10] A character under duress and alone in a room, alone in an existential rather than social sense, is the archetypal image that has always fascinated Pinter: "I think then it might be right to say that I'm dealing with these characters at the extreme edge of their living, where they are living pretty much alone."[11]

How then, it might be asked, does this "image" arise, and how does the play get under way? The first part of the question is not too difficult to answer. It is on record that with such early plays as *The Room, The Birthday Party, The Caretaker,* and *The Homecoming* the initial impulse came from an actual encounter, mostly firsthand, or by anecdote. This incident then sinks into the subconscious and is usually forgotten as time passes, though when combined with some dormant yet selective part of the imagination it is not lost, as, after whatever period of time it takes, the image reappears and the first line of the dialogue is spoken. Of the two men in *The Basement* (1967), for example, Pinter remarked that they had been in his mind for twenty years before he wrote the play. For the play to develop further image has to "engender" image. This process of "engendering" was repeatedly referred to by Pinter in early interviews and statements. In a reply to Peter Wood's request for more explanatory dialogue, Pinter explained to him, as first director of *The Birthday Party,* that the play "was determined by its own original engendering image"[12] of the kitchen set with Meg, Petey, breakfast cornflakes, and so on. In a speech at the National Student Drama Festival at Bristol in 1962 Pinter again described part of the creative process, "where image can freely engender image."[13] The diction here evidently recalls lines from two of W. B. Yeats's most famous poems, "Byzantium" and "Leda and the Swan": "Those images that yet / Fresh images beget," "A shudder in the loins engenders there / The broken wall." Pauline Flanagan, the Irish actress who toured with Anew McMaster, mostly playing juvenile leads opposite Pinter, recalled, "He was also mad about Yeats, and I think Yeats was highly influential."[14]

In this process from authorial subjectivity to the realized objectivity of the character, a kind of autonomy takes over in language, character, and situation, as if Pinter were not the creator but, instead, the recorder of what takes place: "I think a double thing happens. You arrange *and* you listen, following the clues you leave for yourself, through the characters."[15] It is a somewhat Pirandellian situation reminiscent of *Six Characters in Search of an Author* (1921). In Pirandello's play six "characters" wander into a rehearsal seeking full realization, as their author had abandoned them half-conceived. Pinter's characters are absorbed as images, incubated by the subconscious, and then they reassert themselves and take a dramatic life. One way of reading *A Kind of Alaska* (1981) is to see it as almost a precise analogue of Pinter's creative process. This peculiar autonomy, which very much anticipates the structuralist view of art as independent from the author, took an extreme form in Pinter's speech accepting the Hamburg Shakespeare prize: "It may sound absurd, but I believe I am speaking the truth when I say that I have suffered two kinds of pain through my characters. I have witnessed *their* pain when I am in the act of distorting them, of falsifying them, and I have witnessed their contempt. I have suffered pain when I have been unable to get to the quick of them." Most Pirandellian of all, Pinter acknowledged: "I am aware, sometimes, of an insistence in my mind. Images, characters, insisting upon being written."[16]

Such a view should not be taken as an affectation. Put simply, when Pinter begins writing, he doesn't know from the outset where it will end up, and perhaps mistakes can be made. In writing *The Caretaker,* for example, at one stage Pinter thought that the old tramp Davies would be killed by one of the brothers. But, as the writing advanced, it became apparent to him that this couldn't possibly be the case. In an "overview" of Pinter's writing it is possible to discern a fundamental structure, with some variations, in most of the plays and to a certain extent in some of the films. Initially, within a domestic situation two people, or two sides, are found. With exposition largely denied, the subjective relationship is unclear to the audience, and often to the characters, though the attempt by one to exercise some form of influence over the other is apparent. A third character, or characters, in person or by report, is introduced, thereby expanding the structure to a triangular form, which offers dramatic permutation with the following interaction of one person usually siding with one character then another. Pinter generally prefers a relatively brief time scale to stress the contingent nature of the living moment, with a structural shift dependent on such things as the next sentence, the next glance, or the door to open once more.

After development to a point of stress or conflict Pinter is fascinated by drama generated from duplication with difference. A situation similar to the first half is repeated, but under changed circumstances. In the longer plays such as *The Caretaker* and *Old Times* (1971) this is found in the movement from one act to another. A stage direction at the opening of act 2 of *Old Times* makes this structure visually emphatic: *"The divans and armchair are disposed in precisely the same relation to each other as the furniture in the first act, but in reversed order"* (43). In the second half of a Pinter play the conflict is usually ended by one character defeating another, but a neat moral resolution is not suggested by a comforting denouement. Patterns of duplication, reversal, and circularity culminate in actual or implied questions, not answers. Pinter's endings in part derive from the all-important principle touched on earlier, the question of knowing and being known.

The two major factors qualifying this experience for Pinter are evasion of communication and the difficulty of verification. With the great success of *The Caretaker* Pinter was invited to various interviews in the printed press and on radio and television. On one of the most prestigious television arts programs of the day, *Monitor,* Huw Wheldon, in interviewing Pinter, fell into a trap that was very common in early criticism—the assumption that Pinter's plays were about failure of communication. Pinter immediately offered a significant corrective: "I wouldn't say it was accurate as applied to my own work. I don't think there's an inability to communicate on the part of these characters. It's rather more—that they communicate only too well in one sense. Their tentacles go out very strongly to each other, and I think communication is a very fearful matter to really get to know someone, to participate with someone." Pinter continued by bringing sharply into focus a crucial distinction: "I think what takes place really is more an evasion of communication."[17] In the Bristol speech Pinter developed this idea: "I think that we communicate only too well, in our silence, in what is unsaid, and that what takes place is a continual evasion, desperate rearguard attempts to keep ourselves to ourselves."[18] Pinter's ideas suggest a reinterpretation for his own work of the Chekhovian subtext. Stanislavski, Chekhov's friend, colleague, and director, was also one of the most influential theorists of the theater in the twentieth century, and the concept of the subtext derived from his work on Chekhov's plays. For him the subtext is "the manifest, the inwardly felt expression of a human being in a part, which flows uninterruptedly beneath the words of a text, giving them life and a basis for existing": "It is the subtext that makes us say the words we do in a play."[19] Pinter puts his version in a challengingly paradoxical yet comparable fashion: "There are two silences. One when no word is spoken. The other when perhaps a torrent of language is being employed. This speech is speaking of a language locked beneath it. That is its continual reference. The speech we hear is an indication of that which we don't hear."[20] Chekhov's dialogue was, in part, in reaction to the rhetorical posturing of nineteenth-century drama. Pinter's position is largely

in reaction to the polished articulation of the conventional representation of middle-class characters in repertory theater. In an
early interview Pinter illustrated his point with reference to such
a passage as the "light the kettle," "put on the kettle," debate
between Gus and Ben in *The Dumb Waiter,* and it is further dem-
onstrated in Aston and Davies's discussion of the Buddha in *The
Caretaker.* In the case of both Chekhov and Pinter dramatic theory
and practice concerning thought and speech, character and being, was considerably more complex than, for example, something like that allowed for in the drama of ideas, as in the theater
of Sartre and Shaw.

A concomitant of evading communication is the difficulty
of verification, since the latter cannot be available where the
former is the case. If genuine intercommunication is avoided,
then it is not possible to know the true nature of a given situation. Pinter described speech as "a stratagem to cover nakedness"[21]—nakedness, that is, in the metaphorical sense of
vulnerability through exposure both to others and to ourselves.
Speech, in some instances, is like dress, an outward show, and
The Collection (1961), for example, studies the impossibility of
verifying who is lying or telling the truth about a supposed liaison between two dress designers. The memory plays of 1967–
74 enlarged this dimension by dramatizing "the immense
difficulty, if not the impossibility of verifying the past,"[22] as recently as within the past day, let alone years ago.

Whatever the problems of verification, it did seem apparent
to early critics that, with the low-class characters, resonant vernacular, and ordinary rooms, Pinter's first plays could be confi-
dently placed with the contemporary realism associated with

Arnold Wesker and John Osborne. Again Pinter offered a distinction that calls for interpretation because of its ambiguous formulation: "I'd say that what goes on in my plays is realistic, but what I'm doing is not realism."[23] Although Pinter denies a direct affinity with 1950s "kitchen-sink" realism in art and literature, he implies realism of another order.

Pinter's early work coincided with the onset of lower-class regionalism in fiction, onstage, and in film, with such figures as Shelagh Delaney (*A Taste of Honey* [1958]), Alun Owen (*Progress to the Park* [1959]), John Braine (*Room at the Top* [1957]), and Alan Sillitoe (*Saturday Night, Sunday Morning* [1958]; *The Loneliness of the Long-Distance Runner* [1959]). This movement was very important in Britain for the development of television drama, and Pinter's *A Night Out* (1960) made a specific kind of contribution to this. Yet the dramatist was unwilling to concede the identification with the realism of his contemporaries. It is true that the sets for most of Pinter's early plays duplicate the material reality of lower-class life and are consonant for the most part with the speech and dress of the characters. Lower-class realism came about by ramified reasons, but largely in reaction to the below stairs–below decks condescension in the conventional depiction of ordinary people in a culture dominated by idealized representation of middle-class values. This culture had, in turn, inherited a version of ultimately neoclassical prescription in which class prescribed role: the highborn played tragedy, while the low played comedy. The implicit assumption of 1950s realism was that there was a direct relationship between characters and environment, that one reflected the other. In this respect its antecedents derive from the powerful nineteenth-century movement known as French naturalism, as associated with Zola. Pinter, in contrast, is fascinated by the disjunction between the two—between the seemingly concrete external reality of rooms and the reality of individual experience, as far as it can be known. That is to say, Pinter further perceives a dramatic potential in the disparity between the social and existential identities of a character—not what a person is in terms of the labels society unavoidably attaches ("working-class Jew," "middle-class university lecturer," etc.) but, rather, what a person becomes in the mold of experience, the routine and habit of life, "the great deadener," as Beckett called it. Habit in relation to language is central and will take on a particular importance in discussion of Pinter's revue sketches.

Pinter has frequently remarked that he never thinks about his subjects in any kind of abstract way, yet his early technique of juxtaposing the banal and pedestrian with the bizarre and frightening aligns him with one of the foremost theoreticians of the twentieth century. Viktor Shklovsky, associated with the 1920s school of Russian formalism, developed the concept of "defamiliarization," or "making strange," now perhaps remembered in Brecht's use of the "alienation effect" in his theory of the modern epic theater. Shklovsky believed that unreflective immersion in the everyday world renders people insensitive to what should be most familiar. Defamiliarization consisted of whatever artistic techniques are necessary to arrest audience or reader perception of the customary in order to see it afresh. By seemingly stepping outside the norms of rational and articulate language in the registers of theatrical convention, Pinter, more than anybody, defamiliarizes speech and makes an audience feel that it is hearing something for the first time when, in fact, it has always been there. This elemental strangeness in familiarity would have been an inherent part of Pinter's life for many years when, as itinerant actor, he regularly encountered the contrast between the actualities of lodgings, lodgers, landladies, and the like and the relative stylization known as "realism" he was engaged in onstage.

The realists of the 1950s used an explicit dramatic form for what they saw as the explicit dramatic depiction of social and moral issues of class and conduct. Pinter feels that the relating of background facts, items of biography, and so on which conventionally appear in first-act exposition is a form of cheating. Life simply isn't like that. Pinter's preference is usually for a very brief time span in his plays which emphasizes immediacy and confrontation and evades the necessity for causal linkage, which a concatenated series of events would call for. The most dominant received dramatic form was that of "the well-made play," as it was called. Deriving from the extreme formalization of the popular nineteenth-century mode, the well-made play had nevertheless influenced both Ibsen and Chekhov, who largely bestowed it on the twentieth century by way of modification and adaptation. The conventions of the form insisted on exposition, development, complication, catastrophe, and denouement. The mechanics might vary here and there, but the overall conventions were pervasive, stressing overt cause and effect, for speedy action in a melodramatic situation leading to a sensational close.

Although in some respects he is a conventional playwright—providing curtain lines, for example, and mostly writing with the proscenium arch stage in mind—Pinter refuses to provide an exposition or explicit denouement. He sees absence of exposition as itself a source of drama in the unsettling question it raises in the audience as well as onstage. The neat moral and aesthetic resolution of the denouement seems, like the exposition, to run contrary to how life actually is. Pinter opposes explicit form, since it is contrary to the central principle of his view of life and art: ambiguity. "The core of our living . . . this ambiguity,"[24] he once remarked. Paradoxically, Pinter felt that the film of *The Caretaker,* with its opened-out reality of north London snow, sleet, streets, and houses, made the ambiguity of the characters' relationships clearer, whereas the stage production had encouraged an allegorical reading with the critics' insistence on reading character as symbol.[25] Thus, the characters of *The Caretaker* were variously interpreted in Freudian, Marxist, and theological terms as, respectively, the struggle between ego, superego, and id; the class war arising from dialectical materialism; and the Old and New Covenants. In response to such views Pinter remarked, "When a character cannot be comfortably defined or understood in terms of the familiar, the tendency is to perch him on a symbolic shelf, out of harm's way."[26] For Pinter the meaning of a play largely resides in the experience of the play in performance, and to intellectualize that by abstract symbolism is by no means to enrich but, in fact, to impoverish the power of the work.

There was, however, a core of agreement among the early critics, who were, for the most part, reviewers expected to provide an understanding for a paying readership. If symbolic readings diverged widely, in effect a critical truce was arrived at by an agreement on the apparent thematic content of Pinter's plays.

Evasion of communication and the difficulty of verification have already been touched on. The relationship between power and subservience is almost an all-informing concern of Pinter's, parallel with friendship and betrayal, though this equally dominant preoccupation went entirely unnoticed by the early critics, who virtually echoed one another within the parameters of early interpretative stakes. Isolation and alienation linked with contemporary European absurdism, or so it seemed. The territorial imperative in possession and dispossession seemed to offer a social parallel to that of natural history. Perhaps most notoriously, the menace, violence (or threat of violence), and hostility always gave critics a redoubt to fall back into, though this combined with the evident comedy often gave some discomfort.

Leonard Russell, the *Sunday Times* book reviewer, published an open letter to Pinter expressing his dismay at a performance of *The Caretaker* during which he felt patronizing laughter was directed at an ultimately tragic reading of life. Pinter's reply acknowledged that the comic and the tragic are closely interwoven and concluded: "*The Caretaker* is funny up to a point. Beyond that point it ceases to be funny, and it was because of that point that I wrote it."[27] To understand Harold Pinter's plays it is necessary to recognize that "point" as fully as possible. This overview has raised many fundamental issues concerning Pinter's work, and, obviously, not everything could be raised within the confines of this format. In the critical survey that follows many of these issues will be developed with the conviction that understanding Harold Pinter involves understanding society as the twentieth century draws to a close.

Notes

1. "The Rising Generation—A Playwright—Harold Pinter," interview with John Sherwood, 3 March 1960, BBC transcript, 2.

2. "The 22 from Hackney to Chelsea: A Conversation with Harold Pinter" (with Barry Davis), *Jewish Quarterly* (Winter 1991–92): 10.

3. *Ibid.,* 11.

4. "Joseph Brearley, 1909–1977," *Collected Poems and Prose* (London: Faber, 1991), 46.

5. *New Yorker,* 25 February 1967; quoted in William Baker and Stephen Ely Tabachnick, *Harold Pinter* (Edinburgh: Oliver and Boyd, 1973), 11.

6. The practice adopted here will be to give the first production date when a work is mentioned for the first time. The chronology of Pinter's work gives the dates of writing, production, and publication.

7. *New Theatre Magazine* 11, pt. 3 (May–June 1971): 3.

8. *Beckett at Sixty* (London: Calder and Boyars, 1967), 86.

9. "A Conversation [Pause] with Harold Pinter," reprinted in *Critical Essays on Harold Pinter,* edited by Steven H. Gale (Boston: G. K. Hall, 1990), 18.

10. "Rising Generation," 4.

11. "Interview with Harold Pinter" (with Kenneth Tynan), 28 October 1960, BBC transcript, pt. 2, 3.

12. "A Letter to Peter Wood," in *Harold Pinter: "The Birthday Party," "The Caretaker," and "The Homecoming,"* edited by Michael Scott (London: Macmillan, 1986), 79.

13. "Writing for the Theatre," *Plays One* (London: Faber, 1991), xiii.

14. *Harold Pinter: A Casebook,* edited by Lois Gordon (New York and London: Garland, 1990), 234.

15. "Writing for the Theatre," xiii.

16. "Speech: Hamburg 1970," *Theatre Quarterly* 1 (1971): 4.

17. *Monitor,* 5 June 1960, BBC transcript, 3.

18. "Writing for the Theatre," xiii.

19. Constantin Stanislavski, *Building a Character* (London: Methuen, 1968), 113.

20. "Writing for the Theatre," xiii.

21. *Ibid.*

22. *Ibid.,* ix.

23. "Writing for Myself," *Plays Two* (London: Faber, 1991), ix.

24. "New Comment," interview with Laurence Kitchin, 8 October 1963, BBC transcript, 10.

25. *Ibid.,* 8.

26. "Writing for the Theatre," ix.

27. See Ronald Knowles, "The Caretaker and the 'Point' of Laughter"; reprinted in Scott, *Harold Pinter,* 146–61.

CHAPTER TWO

Plays, 1957–60 (I):
The Room, The Dumb Waiter, The Birthday Party, A Slight Ache, A Night Out

The Room (1957)

In this first, one-act play a middle-aged woman, Rose Hudd, garrulously tends to the teatime needs of her totally silent husband, Bert, who is absorbed in a magazine. The modest bed-sitting-room set, speech, and clothing all indicate lower-class ordinariness in what appears to be a scene of dramatic genre painting. Yet something seems amiss. Rose's very insistence on the comparative comforts of the room belies conviction. Her nervous repetition reveals a subtextual fear of being left alone in the room. This insecurity is then increasingly compounded by an incremental dramatic pattern of doubt, indeterminacy, contradiction, and nightmare, from verbal querulousness, ultimately, to blindness and brutality.

Rose is uncertain of who lives elsewhere in the house, particularly in the basement. Mr. Kidd, who drops in somewhat nervously, seems partly deaf to her questions, is reluctant to confirm whether he is the landlord or not and whether he is Jewish or not, and seems uncertain about his room and exactly how many floors the house has. After his departure a peculiar couple call, Toddy and Clarissa Sands, whose upper-class names are quite at odds with their working-class speech. Already unsettled by Mr. Kidd, Rose's insecurity is shaken even further when she hears that they have been told that her room is vacant. Finally, Mr. Kidd returns to reveal that a mysterious figure in the basement has been waiting for some time for Bert to leave so that he may see Rose. Then he enters—a "blind Negro" with a message for Rose, addressed as Sal, from her father, to come home. Bert reenters and kicks the Negro to death, or unconsciousness. Rose becomes blind.

Riley, the Negro, is usually taken as a symbolic figure of death in readings that stress the surreal aspect of the play. This approach tends toward an allegorical view of Rose standing for the compulsive need for security in a hostile world, which can only be ultimately false when measured against the reclamation of mortality. Here it seemed that Pinter had made a British contribution to the contemporary mode known as the theater of the absurd. "Absurdism" refers to the work of such playwrights as Ionesco, Beckett, Arrabal, and Adamov.[1] *The Bald Prima Donna* (1950) and *Waiting for Godot,* (1952) by the first two, respectively, are perhaps the best-known examples. In short, it is considered that these antihumanist, antirealist, nihilist studies in futility in reaction to the atrocity of the war reflect the necessary absurdity of man's godless situation, left to the laughter of preposterous hysteria or the comedy of Stoic resignation.

It is true that at one point Pinter did recall seeing one of Ionesco's plays: "When I wrote *The Birthday Party* I had only seen one of [Ionesco's] plays, *The New Tenant*."[2] This was al-

most certainly the first performance at the Arts Theatre Club,
November 1956, one year before *The Room* was written. The
influence of the first half of *The New Tenant* (*Le nouveau
locataire*) on the first half of *The Room* is striking. In Ionesco's
play an old concierge rambles on unceasingly to the silent new
tenant. But there the formal and stylistic influence ends. In
Ionesco's work the new tenant begins to receive his furniture,
which eventually clogs up the room, the street, and all of Paris in
a striking, yet heavy-handed, symbol of claustrophobic materialism. In contrast, for all the symbolism of the Negro, in *The
Room* and all his plays, Pinter never completely forsakes reality
for symbolic, surreal, or expressionist modes. While originating
in specific historical circumstances, the moral, philosophical, and
religious implications of absurdism, coupled with its antirealist
basis, have tended to encourage abstract symbolic readings, which
regrettably often reduce dramatic richness to an arid formula.

In placing *The Room* in its historical circumstances, it will
be seen that a much more precise and concrete interpretation
emerges. This historicizing of a work of art derives from the
direction taken in recent years by the two "schools" of cultural
theory known as new historicism in the United States and cultural materialism in Great Britain. Both seek to identify the relationship between a work of art and the ideological structure of a
given social formation of which it is a part. Neither the individual nor society can be free from shaping ideological forces,
and, as these critics openly exhibit their political position, so
they strive to uncover the historically inscribed formation in a
work of art.

More modestly here, by reexamining such historical contexts as postwar racism, the cold war, Britain's colonialist inher-

itance, and the class structure of the 1950s, understanding of both *The Room* and *The Birthday Party* may be seen in a fresh light.

Consider the figure of the blind Negro Riley. It should be remembered that, unlike the United States, in Britain before the 1950s black people were mostly found in the dock areas of cities like London, Liverpool, and Cardiff, where they lived and intermarried in contained communities, before the social mobility of the post-1950s era. In part Shelagh Delaney's *A Taste of Honey* (1958) confronted the issue of race relations in the brief romantic idyll of a black Liverpudlian sailor and the heroine yet evaded the outcome by a sentimental resolution. The relationship between Pinter's play and society is altogether more complex. Only a few miles from the newly formed Hampstead Theatre Club, the venue for its first London production, racial tension was building up into what was to be the major race riot of the postwar years. Full employment in the 1950s led to increased West Indian immigration, particularly, which gave rise to overtly social and economic pressures in the big cities, culminating with the Notting Hill race riots of 1958 in London. There were several prevailing attitudes by whites toward blacks in the period, from toleration to extreme racism. *The Room,* in an oblique microcosmic fashion, shared this milieu. Riley the Negro might well be symbolic, but for a contemporary audience he was also very real, the reality of black encroachment beyond identifiable ghettos, like that of Brixton in south London, to white neighborhoods. But Pinter draws on this social fact for psychological ends. As a blind black man, Riley embodies the foreign, the alien, and the bereft, and, as such, he objectifies Rose by symbolizing the condition she hides from herself but inadvertently reveals to the audience. Riley's "Sal" bestows a new identity on Rose, apparently on behalf of her "father." Evidently, this is an existential, not familial, identity of her mind symbolized by the blindness she takes on after ritualizing recognition by touching Riley's eyes prior to Bert's attack.

To an audience of 1957 the transference of Riley's blindness/identity to Rose by way of her touching *"his eyes, the back of his head and his temples"* (109) would have been deeply shocking not only for its symbolic reversal of identity but also in the sexual implications of its tenderness. Pinter has reversed a stereotype. Blacks were supposed to show deference before their colonialist "superiors." Immigration had revealed alarmingly the deep racial prejudice in British society which led to the violence and bloodshed of the riots and left black people fearful in their homes. Part of the unnerving experience of *The Room* is Pinter's covert demonstration that the British were as capable of persecuting a racial minority as anyone else. Economic and social objections to blacks masked the atavistic impulse to punish a scapegoat in place of whatever deep-seated malaise impelled the crowd. With Bert's murderous assault on Riley he screams, "Lice!" (110), a word not used against blacks in the period but one of the images used by Nazi anti-Semitic propaganda to convince themselves of Jewish infestation—a context hinted at when Riley's head is kicked against a gas oven.

Pinter resorted to psychic blindness several times in early plays, giving rise to the charge of symbolic mannerism, which precluded critics from thinking through the deeper implications. In addition, Pinter's first play seemed to show him as a master of merely idiomatic surface. But speech like Rose's in the first half of the play had never been heard before outside comedy. The accuracy of Pinter's behaviorist tonal register made audiences listen in a way they had never been called upon to do in a context that was not just comic but also, ultimately, serious.

The Dumb Waiter (1957)

While in part drawing on a gangster motif, *The Dumb Waiter,* another one-act play, made plain the introduction of an aspect of individual and social experience which was to remain with Pinter throughout his writing career: the role of power and subservience in relationships. Certainly, power features in *The Room* to some extent in the silent domination of Bert as Rose ministers to his needs, but in *The Dumb Waiter* it is central to the drama. Ernest Hemingway's short story "The Killers" was developed into a full-length film by the director Richard Siodmak in 1946, and the opening sequence of two gangsters' shadowy descent on the restaurant deeply impressed Pinter. In the story the laconic ex-prizefighter accepts his end when warned that two gunmen are awaiting him in his local diner, where they hold the staff at gunpoint after a brief contretemps about the menu.

Pinter delays the revelation of Gus and Ben's lethal business until well into the play, when Gus suddenly pulls a revolver from under a pillow. Up until that point Pinter took a bizarre hint from Hemingway—"In their tight overcoats and derby hats they looked like a vaudeville team"[3]—and developed it by using the common revue sketch base of one person reading from a newspaper, together with a comic and stooge cross-talk act, anticipating Goldberg and McCann in *The Birthday Party*. Until the appearance of the revolver they could be comedians and the "organization" they work for a theatrical agency, "Wilson" an impresario, and the "job" a booking in Birmingham. Heretofore, the comedy reproduces that of the cross-talk dominant partner and the querulous sidekick, until a mysterious envelope of matches is slipped under the door, spurring Gus to get his revolver and check outside the door. From this juncture the tone shifts, and an uneasy sense of threat and menace begins to develop in the "light the kettle" sequence (referred to in the overview). It is given extensively here as an illustration of a major aspect of Pinter's comic and yet dramatic mode.

BEN: Go and light it.
GUS: Light what?
BEN: The kettle.
GUS: You mean the gas.
BEN: Who does?
GUS: You do.
BEN: (*his eyes narrowing*). What do you mean, I mean the gas?
GUS: Well, that's what you mean, don't you? The gas.
BEN: (*powerfully*). If I say go and light the kettle I mean go and light the kettle.
GUS: How can you light a kettle?
BEN: It's a figure of speech! Light the kettle. It's a figure of speech!
GUS: I've never heard it.
BEN: Light the kettle! It's common usage!
GUS: I think you've got it wrong.

BEN: (*menacing*). What do you mean?
GUS: They say put on the kettle.
BEN: (*taut*). Who says?
They stare at each other, breathing hard.

(125)

In an early interview Pinter gave this as an example of oblique yet powerful communication: "They deliberately go into this argument as an evasion of the issue. The issue being that they are both in fact frightened of their condition, of their situation, or their state."[4] From this point the comic and the frightening vie in extremes and work upon the audience in a way that Pinter was to exploit throughout his work, as will be discussed particularly in connection with *The Birthday Party.* Here, by way of a dumbwaiter, the two professional killers, while awaiting their victim, receive orders requesting incongruous dishes. Metaphorically, however, Ben is also a dumbwaiter who embodies the unquestioning need for authority, which insists on the unequivocal nature of words and things. Everything has its due function and order for Ben: the car, the newspaper, the lavatory cistern, the kettle. When Gus queries the car's halt, the bizarre stories in the newspaper, the malfunctioning cistern, the issue of lighting the gas or lighting the kettle, the order of things is threatened for Ben. For Gus the provision of matches without an adequate supply of gas implicitly undermines the credibility of the "organization." But for Ben, however bizarre the orders carried by the dumbwaiter, they must do their best to provide something. Gus questions power; Ben conforms to it. Reexamining the play in historicist terms, it can be seen that Ben's criminality is no more than what had been state-authorized in the Europe of the 1930s and 1940s. Unquestioning conformism to authority— not for what authority actually represents but for authority as an absolute in itself—is the ethic of fascism and communism, in which orders are sacrosanct regardless of what the orders actually are. Ben, as "senior partner," reasserts his authority and will kill Gus, who is, in fact, the awaited victim.

The Birthday Party (1957)

"Comedy of Menace" was the subtitle of a 1950s play by David Campton and was taken by Irving Wardle to name an article that became a landmark, in *Encore,* the outstanding avant-garde British theater magazine of the day, in September 1958. A more recent label is "Black Comedy." These critical signposts point toward what some have found to be the almost insurmountable difficulty of the relationship between the comic and the serious in Pinter's plays, particularly in *The Birthday Party,* which is stressed here because in the literary criticism of Pinter's work the comedy is almost entirely discounted.

As a young actor in the 1950s, Pinter found himself wandering along the Eastbourne promenade looking for digs. Eventually, an old deck chair attendant took him to some rather seedy premises. As Pinter recorded in a letter at the time, "I have filthy insane digs, a great bulging scrag of a women with breasts rolling at her belly, an obscene household, cats, dogs, filth, tea strainers, mess, oh bullocks, talk, chat rubbish shit scratch dung poison infantility, deficient order in the upper fret work,"[5] and so on.

Furthermore, in an interview Pinter mentioned an odd encounter in the lodgings: "[I] had to share a room with a man in a kind of attic, sleeping in a bed which had a sofa above it. The sofa was upside down, almost against the ceiling, and I was under the sofa, and he was in the other bed . . . and it was all incredibly dirty. And at the end of the week I said to this fellow, who turned out to have been a concert pianist on the pier: 'Why do you stay here?' And he said 'There's nowhere else to go.'"[6]

Evidently, this was the "engendering" image for the story of Stanley the seedy lodger, Petey and Meg, and the outlandish visitors who arrive and carry off the quondam pianist after terrorizing him at a birthday party. Note, however, that there is no mention in Pinter's letter of figures like Goldberg and McCann. *The Birthday Party* is an amalgam of cultural influences, and the prepossessing Jew and lugubrious Irishman derive from the "lowbrow" mores of the music hall cross-talk act. Comparison of some of Stanley's speeches with the delivery of Tony Hancock has always been made. By the mid-1950s Alan Galton and Ray Simpson's scripts and Hancock's comic genius had made "Hancock's Half Hour" the most successful comedy on radio, as it was to become on television. In contrast, the "highbrow" influence of Kafka's *Trial* is also palpably felt: "K," Kafka's hero, is arrested on his birthday, endures interrogation by two tormentors, and is finally executed, all for an assumed offense, which is never discovered. In many respects *The Birthday Party,* Pinter's first three-act play, reapplies the source for *The Dumb Waiter,* Hemingway's short story "The Killers," but crossed with a play from the "middlebrow" culture of the repertory theater, namely J. B. Priestley's *Mr. Kettle and Mrs. Moon,* which Pinter acted in during the 1950s.[7] In this a rebellious bank manager refuses to go to work and, as a gesture of defiance, buys some children's toys, including a drumstick, which is used on a coal scuttle in time to music. A hypnotist doctor visits the manager, who is seemingly brainwashed as he reappears in the banker's uniform of bowler, black coat, and pinstripe trousers—Stanley's dress, in fact, at the close of the unrevised first version of *The Birthday Party. Lowbrow, highbrow,* and *middlebrow* are terms that, now passed into history, were much used in the 1950s. Pinter's synthesis, however, proved too much for the first London audience at the Lyric Hammersmith, though the play had achieved some success in the provinces, and Harold Hobson's percipient tribute appeared a day after its close: "Mr. Pinter . . . possesses the most original, disturbing and arresting talent in theatrical London," he wrote.[8]

In the 1960 television broadcast the play was not rejected but deeply impressed the millions who avidly discussed it the following day. The theater audience had conventional expectations of the well-made play, while most of the television audience would have been new to drama itself, and *The Birthday Party* obviously worked on its own terms.

At the outset a revue sketch situation provides a basis for comedy combined with 1950s realism. Revue sketches are usually short, four- or five-minute comic presentations that explore the humorous possibilities of everyday encounters. Further discussion will examine their importance for the development of Pinter's art. At the beginning of *The Birthday Party* is found a conventional revue sketch setting of reader, newspaper, and listener. Given, however, the contemporary school of realist painters—John Bratby was the most famous of the day—Pinter was inevitably grouped with the kitchen-sink playwrights. As these painters turned from subjects of politeness and "taste," so contemporary dramatists turned from the genteel drawing rooms of the repertory stage of such writers as Noel Coward and Agatha Christie to the everyday, ordinary, and lower class.

Thus, Petey reads his paper in this seaside boardinghouse, while Meg putters about with breakfast things. The dialogue confirms the sketch possibilities.

> MEG: What are you reading?
> PETEY: Someone's just had a baby.
> MEG: Oh, they haven't! Who?
> PETEY: Some girl.
> MEG: Who, Petey, who?
> PETEY: I don't think you'd know her.
> MEG: What's her name?
> PETEY: Lady Mary Splatt.
>
> (5)

The comic tenor recalls contemporary comedy, but after his entry the occasionally hysterical outbursts of the fractious lodger, Stanley, begin to compromise audience response.

With the entry of Goldberg and McCann the audience is compromised even further. Immediately, a version of the music hall cross-talk act is introduced, with Goldberg as the articulate, outlandish stage Jew and McCann the mournful Irish stooge. Here theatricality compromises realism further. Yet given the deadly mission of the pair to abduct and possibly kill Stanley, a further stratification of genre is found with echoes of the gangster movie—hit men and target, avengers and betrayer—and the Hitchcock domestic thriller. At another extreme Pinter's poem of 1958, "A View of the Party," offers an expressionist perspective—"The thought that Goldberg was / Sat in the center of the room"[9]—as if the intruders were objectifications of Stanley's mind. Pinter has allowed publication of some two dozen poems from his early youth, which were supplemented recently by *Ten Early Poems,*[10] all testifying to the writer's apprenticeship to poetry of the 1940s, particularly that of Dylan Thomas. Elsewhere in the collected verse, in sporadic later poems, are heard voices that were to eventually find dramatic life: "Afternoon," with its pained surreal obliquity, could have been written by the paranoid Len of *The Dwarfs;* "Poem" ("I walked one morning with my only wife") has the accents of the aging Rumsey in *Silence;* while "Message" ("You're sometimes nothing but a walking shithouse") echoes the sardonic Foster of *No Man's Land,* two years earlier. "Later" of 1974 seems to cast a crepuscular reflection on *Moonlight.*

The incongruity of such diverse elements in *The Birthday Party,* however, is never allowed to settle permanently into a synthesized dramatic mode. Sudden shifts intercut between farce, thriller, music hall, domestic realism, melodrama, menace, and comedy. Thus, in the course of the play laughter is provoked by what is ultimately frightening. And this disjunction widens until finally, with the circularity of the conclusion, that which initially created comedy no longer causes laughter. The comic thus, in an increasingly subliminal fashion, induces a feeling of guilt (a correlative to the postwar situation, it will be argued). For example, consider the effect of the contrast between the end of

UNDERSTANDING HAROLD PINTER

act 1 and the opening of act 2. The "*savage and possessed*" (30) beating of the drum is succeeded by McCann's tearing of the newspaper into "*five equal strips*" (31), which has several functions. From the point of view of performance it is usually done, taking the verbal cues that follow, with manic intensity. It is bizarre, faintly ludicrous, and thus a touch comic. Yet the intensity makes an audience apprehensive. The conversational exchanges between McCann and Stanley seem to lessen this, but then, as McCann actually prevents Stanley from leaving the room, the succeeding exchanges of conventional introduction are made even more alarming because the audience is now aware that this belies a more threatening reality. They then begin a mock battle, which is often dropped in performance, a whistling competition to the tune of "The Mountains of Mourne." Again the bizarre works both ways, comic yet menacing, which checks and compromises responses. McCann again blocks Stanley's exit and reacts with suppressed violence when Stanley picks up one of the strips of paper. Instead of allowing a steady buildup to a violent climax, Pinter reverts from the mixed mode to alternation, and comedy takes over, at least on the surface.

> STANLEY: Ever been anywhere near Maidenhead?
> McCANN: No.
> STANLEY: There's a Fuller's teashop. I used to have my tea there.
> McCANN: I don't know it.
> STANLEY: And a Boots Library. I seem to connect you with the High Street.
> McCANN: Yes?
> STANLEY: A charming town, don't you think?

(33)

Could anything be less threatening than "Maidenhead," "Fuller's teashop," and "Boots Library"? Such a roll call finds comedy in the diversionary contrast that provides a form of comic relief (almost like a burlesque of a Hitchcock thriller). Then, in response to McCann's moroseness, Stanley's increasing nervousness leads him to talk too much about himself, culminating in his attempt to put himself over as a hard-drinking tough guy: "Been drinking a bit down here. . . . I mean, you wouldn't think, to look at me, really. . . . I mean, not really, that I was the sort of bloke to—to cause any trouble, would you?" (34). Stanley compounds bluff and self-delusion, which reveal rather than conceal his real weaknesses.

His various appeals to McCann having failed, Stanley's fear grows and, along with it, the audience's sense of guilt at earlier laughter. Stanley abuses the absent Meg, and McCann has to restrain him by force. Developing from McCann's physical attack, Pinter allows the menace to rise and then pricks it and allows an extended deflation in Goldberg's entry and comic celebration, "A mother in a million" (36). Before proceeding to an interpretation that will combine a historicist perspective on the cold war period with an essentially Freudian reading, a further aspect of modern theory will be briefly considered. "Audience reception" in the study of drama studies the interrelationship between play, performance, and audience, looking at historical situation, particular social occasion, the social stratification, and patronage—that is, to find out as much as possible about audiences to see what light it throws on the play. A reassessment of the early audiences of *The Birthday Party* in relation to the resumption of Irish Republican Army (IRA) activity on mainland Britain after the war provides a new perspective on the play.[11]

A few key quotations focus on the subject—McCann: "Why did you leave the organization. . . . Why did you betray us? . . . You betrayed the organization" (42); Goldberg: "Webber! Why did you change your name?" (44); McCann: "You betrayed our land" (46); Goldberg: "You betrayed our breed" (46); Meg: "He's been here about a year now" (25). Last, Stanley, having lived in Maidenhead (33) and Basingstoke (36), the same town "just outside" of which we are told that Goldberg's Uncle Barney had a house (21), takes on a less than innocent significance when the details are assembled.

The first major IRA raid on mainland Britain after the war was that on Felstead School Officers Training Corps armory, in Essex on 25 July 1953, which received national press coverage. The leader John Stephenson was charged as Sean Stephenson, also known as Seán MacStiofáin, and was known to have used other aliases. It was believed that "a fourth man" had gone to ground. Two years on, and closer to *The Birthday Party,* a more dramatic raid on the Royal Electrical and Mechanical Engineering (REME) army depot took place, at Arborfield in Berkshire. This raid gave rise to alarm at the enemy within and without, as throughout the country it was rumored that bombs had been planted in places of entertainment, one of which was the Hippodrome Theatre in Wolverhampton. Just when Pinter was working as an actor, the IRA threat was prevalent, particularly for theatergoers. When *The Birthday Party* played at the Hippodrome, in 1958, regulars hearing McCann's charges against Stanley—the "Organization" was a well known euphemism for the IRA—could not have failed to remember an evening three years earlier when the theater had to be searched because of a bomb hoax during a performance. As in a Pinter play, threat and the laughter of relief were found. Arborfield lies exactly half-way between Basingstoke and Maidenhead. Meg's remark, "He's been here about a year now" (25), fits with these details. Pinter wrote the play in 1957 with Stanley in mind as having arrived sometime in 1955–56, directly in the aftermath of the Arborfield raid when many IRA men were known to have fled. Recreation of these particular circumstances adds even more to what must have been the audience response of the day.

Goldberg's reveries, however, lead into the much greater social and psychological depth of the implications of authority and power in *The Birthday Party* compared to that in *The Dumb Waiter*. Organically interrelated image and allusion provide a focus on the link between authority and childhood—namely, the failure of all father figures. Goldberg, McCann, and Stanley are paralleled, in that each are spoiled like little boys: Goldberg by his wife, McCann by "Mother Nolan," Stanley by Meg. In the course of the birthday party all regress under the influence of alcohol, recalling childhood. Lulu treats Goldberg like a father figure. Meg pathetically claims that her party dress was given to her by her father, who, it appears, abandoned her to a children's home, which she fantasizes as a place where doctors and nurses become "Nanny" and "Father" (54).

A father figure is characterized by love and authority, affection and power, which in *The Birthday Party* are divided and reversed, the abstract menace of impersonal authority displacing the personal security of love, here symbolized by the image of the failed or absent father. Stanley's father did not make the concert at Lower Edmonton, and Petey, as a father substitute, fails to prevent Stanley's abduction. Meg was abandoned by her father in childhood. As Uncle Barney was to Goldberg, so Goldberg is to McCann, bringing him "down for a few days to the seaside" (21). Lulu's trust in Goldberg as a father figure is abused. Goldberg becomes a false father to Stanley after validating his bourgeois conformity by invoking his own father.

This psychological reading has social and political correlatives. A core reality of the war was the symbol of the Jew abducted and murdered by "authority." Stanley's torment, breakdown, and abduction reproduces in the audience the guilt of helplessness, which duplicates what was the case when the fate of the Jews was discovered. Here, surrealistically, it is reenacted, and, as in a nightmare, the audience is helpless to prevent it. In the postwar recoil from horror, another Jew returned, the stand-up comedian or cross-talk act. Pinter's hybrid mode crosses not just forms of theater but manifestations of reality as well. The persecuted becomes the persecutor. The source of humor becomes the source of terror. In a letter to the first director of *The Birthday Party* Pinter referred to Goldberg and McCann as "the hierarchy, the Establishment, the arbiters, the socioreligious monsters [who] arrive, affect alteration and censure upon a member of the club who has discarded responsibility."[12] This can be taken further. As grotesque deformations of history, they reclaim the son, Stanley, who must be reborn into the masquerade of normality, the grotesque reality of the postwar world. The authority they represent is the failed father, the leader, the *pater patriae,* "father of his country." (In a recent Oxford Union debate Pinter referred to the United States' self-appointed role as the world's policeman as "the world's dad").[13] These collective leaders—Hitler, Stalin, Mussolini, Franco, Roosevelt, and Churchill—had either inaugurated or failed to prevent the slaughter of the innocent who held them in trust. The image of Abraham and Isaac is more germane than the usual Oedipus comparisons. Like Joyce's hero Stephen Dedalus, Stanley is trying to awaken from the nightmare that is history, but there is no escape from history, or memory, for him or the audience.

In a sense a British audience did escape from one of the worst horrors of the war—namely, occupation and its aftermath of totalitarian police states. From this point of view Pinter applies postwar Continental experience to a British situation, thereby fulfilling the Kafkaesque scenario depicted by no less a figure than Sir Winston Churchill in his first speech as leader of the opposition in the House of Commons, 16 August 1945. Considering the plight of many European countries subject to police governments, he said: "There they [the family] sit. Suddenly there is a knock at the door and a heavily armed policeman appears. . . . It may be that the father or son, or a friend sitting in the cottage, is called out and taken off into the dark, and no one knows whether he will ever come back again, or what his fate has been. All they know is that they had better not enquire."[14]

A Slight Ache (1958)

A Slight Ache once again features an intruder who brings menace and breakdown, both social and psychological, but here, in his choice and treatment of an upper-class setting and characters, Pinter drew on distinct elements of parody for his particu-

lar comic mode. Middlebrow and highbrow culture are burlesqued in the Noel Cowardish elements of drawing room comedy and in the oblique anthropological allusions to Fraser's *The
Golden Bough,* which had underpinned T. S. Eliot's *Waste Land*
(1922).

After the fiasco of the reception of *The Birthday Party* at
the Lyric, Hammersmith, certain British Broadcasting Corpora-
tion (BBC) personnel, and Donald McWhinnie in particular,
thought that the new young writer had been unjustly savaged by
an uncomprehending and dismissive press. McWhinnie had established his credentials with radio productions of Samuel
Beckett, and partly through his advocacy Pinter received a commission from the BBC. *A Slight Ache* was the first result. The
initial slight ache in Edward's eyes and the intrusion of the wasp
in an idyllic summer morning prefigure the entry of the match
seller, whose silent presence releases Edward's wife's, Flora's,
sexual and maternal fantasies (akin to Meg's in *The Birthday
Party*). Flora appropriates the match seller and rejects her husband, whose identity has collapsed before the intruder.

The radio production emphasized the psychological aspect
of the play, while the equally successful stage version inevitably
shifted the focus onto the social aspects of the drama. On radio
the silent match seller became the catalyst for psychological pro-
jections of power conflict between Flora's sexuality and Edward's
intellectuality, as if he were an invention in a game played between them comparable to that in *The Lover.* The unseen match
seller promotes an overt psychoanalytical reading of symbolic
impotence which can somewhat obscure the wider social reverberations Pinter pointedly makes in the play.

The pastoral scene of timelessness ("the longest day of the year" [154]), with seemingly anachronistic allusion ("the three masted schooner" [179]), invokes a context wider than the literal. Edward's polymathic intellectual pursuits suggest an early Edwardian figure, while his sporting past, country house cricket matches, and polo suggest upper-class affluence and distance from such a proletarian urban figure as the match seller. Similarly, Flora's past social position, apparently a former justice of the peace, is burlesqued by her fantasies of rape. By a technique of pointed allusion to social contexts going well beyond psychological naturalism, Pinter is able to suggest metaphorical possibilities. Edward and Flora's furniture, it is revealed, was bought in a sale, which implies that their social position is not inherited but acquired. They are parvenu, which somewhat reverses the charge—"impostor" (173)—made by Edward against the match seller.

In social terms Edward embodies the social pretensions of the twentieth-century upper-class English country gentleman, refusing to recognize the reality of postwar change and hiding away in a cocooned rural idyll. The match seller, visibly there onstage, is a haunting image of the 1930s Depression and postwar deprivation. Comedy is used to parody social position, and the prewar cocktail mise-en-scène of a Noel Coward invitation becomes a parody in Edward's offer to the match seller: "What will you have to drink? A glass of ale? Curaçào Fockink Orange? Ginger Beer? Tia Maria? A Wachenheimer Fuchsmantel Reisling Beeren Auslese? Gin and it? Chateauneuf-du-Pape? A little Asti Spumante? Or what do you say to a straightforward Piesporter Goldtropschen Feine Auslese (Reichsgraff von

Kesselstaff)? Any preference?" (169). And just as T. S. Eliot had used such a milieu for the higher seriousness of *The Cocktail Party,* conversely, Pinter imports satiric allusion with Flora as fertility goddess, Edward as dying god, while the match seller tramp, named by Flora after Saint Barnabas, presides over the summer solstice as the new god displacing the old.[15] Pinter's generation was profoundly influenced by Eliot, and comparisons of Pinter's work with *Sweeney Agonistes* are found from time to time. Pinter's comic appropriation of such fertility myths and juxtaposition with the Noel Coward element is worthy of the Menippean satire of a Lucian in the burlesque of modernist symbolism while still making an ultimately serious point.

The match seller's intransigent silence can be taken in social terms as the objectification of the problem of class differentials in mid-twentieth-century Britain which simply would not be wished away. By the late 1950s, when, as Prime Minister Macmillan reminded everybody, "You never had it so good," the working class in the period of reconstruction and reflation was indeed acquiring a way of life which was previously associated exclusively with the middle classes. Yet, inevitably, the poor, like the match seller, are always with us. *A Night Out* provides a perfect study of the lower-middle-class mores of the period.

A Night Out (1960)

With relatively full employment and increasing affluence, particularly after the inauguration of a commercial television channel in 1955, television ownership by 1960 had increased from the 1950 figure of a quarter of a million to ten million. "By

PLAYS, 1957–60 (I)

1959," Robert Hewison writes, "with seven or eight plays a week on the commercial and BBC channels, there was a need for some 400 self-contained plays a year."[16] In 1958 the Canadian Sydney Newman was contracted by ABC television to develop the projected Sunday night series "Armchair Theatre." Newman, deeply influenced by TV series in the United States—"Playhouse 90" and "Play of the Week"—and such founding fathers of TV realism as Paddy Chayefsky (*Marty*) and Rod Serling (*Requiem for a Heavyweight*), set about commissioning Alun Owen, Clive Exton, Harold Pinter, and others.[17]

"Armchair Theater" followed the enormously popular variety show "Sunday Night at the London Palladium." Thus, *A Night Out* was broadcast to an audience of sixteen million, most of whom would have been quite new to serious drama. Social realism of the 1950s as promoted by Newman—"I am proud that I played some part in the recognition that the working man was a fit subject for drama, and not just a comic foil in a play on middle-class manners"[18]—presented the overwhelming majority of the audience of working-class, lower-middle-class, and middle-class people with their own lives, faithfully rendered, and Pinter's *A Night Out* was one of its great successes.

In the opening scenes Pinter evokes a whole world of social entrapment. Albert, dressed in white shirt and "best trousers" (332), cleans his shoes in preparation for an office party. His tie is pressed, and the ubiquitous lounge suit must be brushed before leaving the house, complete with a handkerchief in his breast pocket. Albert is thus transformed into the image of his father: "You've got to be properly dressed. Your father was always properly dressed. You'd never see him without a handkerchief in his breast pocket. He always looked like a gentleman" (341). In microcosm here we have the aspirations of British class mimicry. Broadly speaking, fashions permeated down the social scale, beginning with the aristocracy, which provided the model. Each class takes as its model the one above within a culture yet to be superseded by all that the late 1960s achieved. Thus, Albert appears as that peculiar image of instant middle age, characteristic of the period.

In the television production of *A Night Out* Pinter added a slight but telling detail of fashion and class, a synecdoche for a whole ethos, which is not in the current printed edition. At the office party Albert's associate Seeley congratulates the overbearing Gidney, who eventually victimizes his junior: "That's a lovely pair of elastic sided shoes you're wearing there, Gidney." Such footwear, which was very fashionable in the period, derived directly from the design of the upper-class riding boot.

Albert's mother's emotional coercion, invoking "father" and "Grandma," is just the domestic side of the larger social entrapment of work and play in the hierarchies of football and office which regulate expectation of performance and behavior. Sexuality is socially repressed by the polarized categories of the day— nice girls or loose women—according to which the logical outcome is that premarital sex is unclean: "Are you leading a clean life?" (335), Albert is asked.

After being victimized at the party for a sexual misdemeanor he was innocent of, Albert in turn bosses around a prostitute, who insists on presenting her occupation in the self-deluding language of gentility, thereby presenting a gross travesty of Albert's mother and the idea of breeding pressed home by Gidney (contrast 358 and 365). Comparison with *The Birthday Party* is frequently made. Both Stanley and Albert are marked by social and sexual failure, and both are trapped by mother figures, to whom Albert helplessly returns to be pinioned indefinitely by the wheedling bonds of his mother's final intimidation, her approval and disapproval expressing the impossibility of escaping society's strictures:

> It's not as if you're a bad boy . . . you're a good boy . . . I know you are . . . it's not as if you're really bad, Albert, you're not . . . you're not bad, you're good . . . you're not a bad boy Albert, I know you're not. . . .
> *Pause.*
> You're good, you're not bad, you're a good boy . . . I know you are . . . you are, aren't you? (375)

The marked difference from *The Birthday Party* is in that particular aspect of human ambiguity which Pinter saw as central to his writing: "If I'm being explicit I'm failing."[19] In this respect Albert's motives seem quite clear in comparison with Stanley's behavior. What kind of pianist Stanley might have been remains in doubt, but Albert's conscious imposture before the prostitute as an assistant film director is an obvious compensation for his unglamorous life. Albert's coworker Seeley is crucial here. In what appears to be a spontaneous act of friendship he defends Albert against his attackers, yet his own edgy defensiveness and irritation at the mention of Albert's mother suggest that he suffers from a comparable vulnerability, though it is never stated. Any other dramatist of the day would have realized an affective vignette between the two young men. Instead, in a play free from any kind of distracting symbolism, Pinter provided dialogue with such persuasive vernacular that it remained a memorable part of the play for many, such as the following:

> KEDGE: I bet his Mum's combing his hair for him, eh?
> *He chuckles and sits.*
> You ever met her, Seeley?
> SEELEY: Who?
> KEDGE: His . . . mother.
> SEELEY: Yes.
> KEDGE: What's she like?
> SEELEY: (*shortly*) She's all right.
> KEDGE: All right, is she?
> SEELEY: I told you. I just said she was all right.
> *Pause.*
> KEDGE: No, what I mean is, he always gets a bit niggly, when she's
> mentioned, doesn't he? A bit touchy. You noticed that?
> SEELEY: (*unwillingly*) Yes.
> KEDGE: Why's that, then?
> SEELEY: I don't know. What're asking me for?
> KEDGE: I don't know. I just thought you might . . . sort of . . .
> well, I mean, you know him better than I do, don't you?
> *Pause.*
> Of course, he don't let much slip, does he, old Albert?
> SEELEY: No, not much.
> KEDGE: He's a bit deep really, isn't he?
> SEELEY: Yes, he's a bit deep.

$$(341–42)$$

Ironically, it is Seeley who is "touchy," and only Albert's misfortune nearly causes him to reveal whatever might be behind such speech. But whatever it is remained ambiguous, with

Pinter himself in the original part, seemingly the precise opposite of Tom Bell's Albert—brash, tough, and matey in his social role, otherwise retaining the ambiguity that Pinter saw as the core of his work.

Notes

1. See Martin Esslin, *The Theatre of the Absurd,* rev. ed. (Harmondsworth: Penguin Books, 1968).

2. "Mr Harold Pinter—Avant-Garde Playwright and Intimate Review," *The Times,* 16 November 1959, 4.

3. *Men without Women* (1928; reprint, Harmondsworth: Penguin Books, 1955), 65.

4. "Interview with Harold Pinter," 28 October 1960, BBC transcript, pt. 1, 6.

5. "Harold Pinter: An Interview" (with Lawrence Bensky), in *Pinter: A Collection of Critical Essays,* edited by Arthur Ganz (Englewood Cliffs, N.J.: Prentice-Hall, 1972), 20.

6. "In an Empty Bandstand" (1969), 630.

7. See Leslie Smith, "Pinter the Player," *Modern Drama* 22, no. 4 (1979): 349–63.

8. *Sunday Times,* 25 May 1958, 11.

9. *Collected Poems and Prose,* (London: Faber, 1991), 46.

10. The Greville Press, 1992.

11. For further discussion see Ronald Knowles, "The Road to Basingstoke: *The Birthday Party* and the IRA," *The Pinter Review* (1993).

12. "A Letter to Peter Wood," in *Harold Pinter: "The Birthday Party," "The Caretaker," and "The Homecoming,"* edited by Michael Scott (London: Macmillan, 1986), 82.

13. Typescript courtesy of Harold Pinter.

14. *War Speeches 1939–45,* vol. 3 (London: Cassell & Co, 1952) 519–20.

15. See Katherine H. Burkman, *The Dramatic World of Harold Pinter: Its Basis in Ritual* (Columbus: University of Ohio Press, 1971), 47–64, for a non-comedic reading using this approach.

16. Robert Hewison, *In Anger: Culture in the Cold War, 1945–60* (London: Methuen, 1981), 174.

17. See Irene Shubik, *Play for Today: The Evolution of Television Drama* (London: Davis-Poynter, 1975).

18. *Ibid.,* 40.

19. *The Daily Mail,* 7 March 1964, 8.

CHAPTER THREE

Plays, 1957–60 (II):
The Caretaker, the Revue Sketches,
The Hothouse, Night School, The Dwarfs

The Caretaker (1960)

In *The Caretaker,* contrasting with the preceding two plays, the characters hover on the margins of society. Claiming "I've had dinner with the best" (7), Mac Davies, a tramp, is given shelter by the isolated Aston, who is still suffering from the effects of shock treatment for a mental disorder. The owner of the run-down property they are staying in is Mick, Aston's brother, who self-delusively aspires to the refinement of interior decorator to the upper classes. In terms of action little actually happens in the play. Davies's peculiarly prevaricating opportunism is no match for the complex psychology of the brothers, and, after a two-week stay, he is asked to leave. Yet, in spite of such seeming limitation, *The Caretaker* may be placed with Pinter's greatest achievements and thus among work that has contributed to the development of twentieth-century drama.

While Pinter was renting a Chiswick flat in the late 1950s, the elder of two tenants also in the house, who were brothers, invited back a tramp. In due course, following a row, the tramp was thrown out. Nearby lived an Indian photographer. These bare facts provided the engendering stimulus for Pinter's imagination, which responded immediately. When the play was in rehearsals Donald Pleasance, who established the role of Davies, recalled: "Harold met [the tramp] and discovered he was washing up in the Black and White milk bar. He was last seen crossing Hammersmith Bridge." Pinter acknowledged: "I got some of the lines from this tramp. The rest I took forward in a sort of logical progression."[1]

One kind of manifest progression was, put crudely, from symbolism to realism. In large part *The Caretaker* is a dramatic exploration of the relationship between character and language untrammeled by any kind of symbolic distraction, which many have found in the earlier plays. For this development the early revue sketches are a major turning point in Pinter's development and will be examined shortly. Several times in early interviews Pinter recognized what had taken place. He recorded that "the original idea when writing [was] to end the play with a violent death of the tramp": "[But] it suddenly struck me that it wasn't necessary. And that in the play I personally feel that I have developed, that I have no need to use cabaret turns and black outs and screams in the dark."[2] A new kind of conviction and confidence was evinced in the remarks immediately following: "I feel that I can deal, without resorting to that kind of thing, with a human situation, which I do see this play as being—really a particular human situation concerning three particular people, and not, incidentally, as symbols."[3] When Pinter came across photographs of an early Continental production of the play showing that the concrete details of the detritus of Aston's attic had been symbolically transformed by a gauze that confounded ceiling and sky, thereby conferring a sense of an elemental micro-macrocosmic exposure, he was dismayed. Conversely, he was delighted by the material reality of the film version, which was opened out to include the uncompromising Hackney locale with Davies begging on the streets in the snow, Aston's pond in the garden, and Mick's van parked outside.

To a considerable extent, insistent symbolic readings of modern drama came about because of two primary factors: the heritage of Ibsen's plays and the imperatives of drama reviews. The powerful realism of Ibsen's middle period had included plays like *The Wild Duck* (1884), which found a driving dynamic potential in combining elements of exposition, psychology, and plot, all within the prismatic symbol of the hapless bird. The danger of such a mode is that it can vary from the richly imaginative to the crudely mechanical. Responses to Ibsen varied in his own day, and with this kind of artistic bequest the dangers have remained for successors. For example, some might take the view that, in plays such as Tennessee Williams's *The Glass Menagerie* (1945) and *Suddenly Last Summer* (1958), resorting to animal symbolism was more like reverting to symbolic shorthand, rather than drawing on resources of imagination and experience. The issue is compounded by reviewers pushed for space and time who readily grasp a symbolic handle as the reducible means of seeming to say a lot in a little. Thus, as described in the overview, critics were almost desperate to find some all-encompassing allegorical reading of *The Caretaker* when, in fact, Pinter included, in dramatic form, an implicit critique of his earlier mode. After a lights fade in act 2 Davies fumbles about in the dark with matches because of a seemingly dud light bulb. A suddenly fierce roar of a (usually amplified) machine terrifies both him and the audience. It turns out to be Mick operating a vacuum cleaner, "I was just doing some spring cleaning" (43), he explains.

Any object onstage accrues meaning in a way that it would not do ordinarily in everyday life simply because of exposure to a concentrating audience. Further, such an object may often develop a significance along with what is taking place in the theater. Rather than labeling something "symbolic," which can be supererogatory and detract from dramatic power, it is worth reconsidering aspects of *The Caretaker* in the light of semiology, or the science of signs. Semiology explores the relationship between the sign and the signified within a structure of meaning. Obviously, within human culture language itself is arguably the most complex sign system, but one among others in the ramifications of society—for example, the signifying agency of such things as clothing, food, and the possessions we surround ourselves with or use, not least the motorcar. From one point of view dramatists can hardly fail to be semiological to the extent that, in such matters as set design, objects are likely to take on a function within the totality of a highly structured system like a play.

Objects seen, or unseen, play a large part in *The Caretaker.* Most notoriously, perhaps, Davies's distant unreclaimed "papers" in Sidcup and Aston's ever-to-be-, never-to-be-built shed. The unseen vacuum cleaner has a powerful dramatic function in act 2, as we have seen. Among the junk of the attic the toaster and planks of wood have a particular significance for Aston, complementing that of sandals, shoes, and shirts for Davies.

The objects that tend to dominate the set visibly, however, are the bucket suspended from the ceiling and the Buddha enshrined on the gas stove. At the outset Mick's silent stare draws the attention of the audience to them. Then, halfway through the first act they impinge on the characters. Davies picks up the statue:

DAVIES: What's this?
ASTON: (*taking and studying it*) That's a Buddha.
DAVIES: Get on.
ASTON: Yes, I quite like it. Picked it up in a . . . in a shop.
  Looked quite nice to me. Don't know why. What do you
  think of these Buddhas?
DAVIES: Oh, they're . . . they're all right, en't they?
ASTON: Yes, I was pleased when I got hold of this one. It's very
  well made.

(15–16)

Aston, a would-be "Carpenter" (15), as Davies insists, likes working with his hands and appreciates something well made, though his choice of something religious rather than practical as an example of this is just one more example of behavior that confirms his oddity, like his strangely bewildering anecdote about drinking Guinness from a thick mug.

But, in considering the behavior of language, here an example occurs of what Pinter insisted on as evasion, rather than failure, of communication. Davies initiates the discussion, presumably feeling obliged to ask, rather than having a natural interest. Aston's following remarks deepen the incongruity, since he talks of "picking up" the Buddha "in a shop," much as he has come across Davies in a café. Davies replies to his question, "What do you think of these Buddhas?" with neutrally guarded compliance, "Oh they're . . . they're all right, en't they?" (15). The Buddha provides the possibility of both entering into something other than the mere tangency of encounter, but whatever either really might feel or need—a deeper conscious or unconscious motive in Aston or Davies's nascent crude intuition into Aston's mentality—lies beneath the surface and remains unspoken. In the following sequences literal silence is often structured around the bucket.

In act 1 Davies "*suddenly becomes aware of the bucket and looks up.*" Aston's explanation, taciturn and monosyllabic, is "Leak" (19). But what the bucket comes to signify in dramatic terms is considerably less perfunctory than this. In act 2 attention to the drip into the bucket provides the briefest relief in Mick's intimidation of Davies, which culminates in his comic monologues. At the close of the third monologue Aston reenters, and here for the first time the brothers are together. Many consider *The Caretaker* to be about the relationship of the two brothers, yet they say next to nothing to each other. It is rewarding, therefore, to look closely at what is said, however apparently banal.

Silence.
A drip sounds in the bucket. They all look up.
Silence.
MICK: You still got that leak.

Aston: Yes.
Pause.
    It's coming from the roof.
Mick: From the roof, eh?
Aston: Yes.
Pause.
    I'll have to tar it over.
Mick: You're going to tar it over?
Aston: Yes.
Mick: What?
Aston: The cracks.
Pause.
Mick: You'll be tarring over the cracks on the roof.
Aston: Yes.
Pause.
Mick: Think that'll do it?
Aston: It'll do it, for the time being.
Mick: Uh.
Pause.
Davies: (*abruptly*). What do you do . . . ?
They both look at him.
    What do you do . . . when that bucket's full?
Pause.
Aston: Empty it.

                                                   (35)

    In this section of dialogue the drip occurs between two silences, and there are six further pauses. Such sparsity of utterance follows Mick's forty-two-line monologue. The effect is to suggest the concentrated subtext beneath the actual spoken dialogue, a factor fundamental to Pinter's artistry. His theater gives primacy to language over action as it gives primacy to being over character and then goes one step further, by recognizing a necessary corollary of the evasion of communication in silence itself. Hence the notorious pauses and silences of Pinter's drama, which were to become the favorite butt of unsympathetic critics. For Pinter "the pause is a pause because of what has just happened in the minds and guts of the characters": "And a silence equally means that something has happened to create the impossibility of anyone speaking for a certain amount of time—until they can recover from whatever happened before the silence."[4]

Said acerbically, Mick's dialogue can be taken as expressing simple resentment and frustration with Aston's procrastination. A sardonic edge would imply Mick's doubt that the repair would ever get done, since the bucket is only there as a substitute for what should have been done in the first place. Alternatively, it is possible to express a kind of solicitude to give the lines a developing fraternal coloring. This, however, would entail the sentimental simplicities of a brotherly love reading of the play as a whole. Onstage Alan Bates, the creator of the role, remained largely inscrutable, yet, when he repeated the part for the film version, camera close-ups showed a disturbed and troubled face quite different from his adoption of a comic mask. In studying these lines, it would be a mistake to grant Mick complete self-awareness. For all his playful certainty in the role he adopts before Davies, perhaps he doesn't really know what he feels about his brother and in fact evades facing up to just that. Aston is both his brother and evidently a deeply disturbed human being. Perhaps Mick can accept one, but not the other.

Act 3 immediately picks up in the bucket drip motif. Davies, now sumptuously attired in a smoking jacket, comments on the state of the roof:

> I got a feeling he's done something to those cracks.
> *Pause.*
> See, there's been plenty of rain in the last week, but it ain't
> been dripping into the bucket.
> *Pause.*
> He must have tarred it over up there. (56)

This can be taken in several ways. Aston has done something at last which thereby signals his recovery, a practical activity indicating his mental recuperation; or it could be said that
to tar over a leak is really only a short-term solution, temporarily and provisionally mending something more seriously structural—another form of procrastination, which is a possibly less
optimistic analogy for the real condition of Aston's mind. Of the
tarring job Aston had remarked, "It'll do it, for the time being"
(35). Davies, like Aston, turns the provisional into a permanent
condition of his existence. He thanked Aston for "letting me have
a bit of a rest, like . . . for a few minutes" (8–9), but, as act 3
opens, it becomes apparent that a few minutes have turned into
at least a week. Both are caught on a psychological treadmill
that rises on pragmatism and falls in evasion. In contrast, Mick's
tortured confrontation with himself is by way of the Buddha.

The emotional climax of act 3 occurs with the smashing of
the Buddha; Mick seemingly uses the gesture, in general, as an
expression of his anger at Davies and, in particular, as a fraudu-
lent interior decorator. He pays him off—"Here's half a dollar"—
and then, in response to Davies's "if that's what you want," the
stage direction reads: "*He hurls the Buddha against the gas stove*"
(72). What is most important here is the revised stage direction
of 1962 which immediately follows his action, indicating the

nature of his speech—*"Passionately."* In the first edition of 1960 this read: *"To himself, slowly, broodingly."* With such passion Mick's ironic mask has dropped. Davies's failings are obvious throughout, so Mick's emotional vulnerability has been revealed by something closer to his suppressed feelings, namely Davies's charge that Aston is "nutty." "Did you call my brother nutty? My brother" (71), Mick asks. At that moment the Buddha symbolizes for Mick all that he cannot accept about his brother—his procrastination, his inadequacy, his eccentricity, his unreliability, and, finally, his mental illness. Mick also wants Aston to "live like the others" (53). That is, to be like him, able to take care of himself, in the narrow sense. In the faint smile that they exchange toward the close (73), Mick believes it signals Aston's agreement with his view of things. Aston's last words in rejection of Davies were: "Get your stuff" (67). In addition to this complexity the smashing of the Buddha also acknowledges Mick's own failure not just as a posh interior decorator but also in the recognition of his own self-delusion in the fantasy of elegance he has just rehearsed.

Pinter once recorded, "What I'm interested in is emotion which is contained, and felt very, very deeply . . . perhaps it is ultimately inexpressible."[5] This can be evidently applied to Mick and Aston, where it appears that brotherly love has undergone such social and mental convolutions that it barely recognizes itself. But Pinter's statement also applies to an audience, and this is perhaps in large part why his plays have caused such controversy, though the cause has not always been recognized. In the emotional experience of a play—the experience onstage and in an audience—the audience finally confronts not just the concluding tableau but also its own emotional vulnerability. At least that is arguably the case with Pinter's most complex achievements, including *The Caretaker,* which is brought about by a radical revision of tragedy and comedy, in the constant compromise of audience reaction and the denial of an escape into sentimentalism.

At the outset of his writing career Pinter believed that "the old categories of comedy and tragedy and farce are irrelevant."[6] "Tragedy" simply offers a "life belt" to critics, and "this category business is the most facile of things."[7] The heroic ideal of self-knowledge through suffering is something to which neither Pinter nor Chekhov could subscribe. Black comedy or theater of the absurd appears to be the dramatic response to a century in which the progressive aspect of the Enlightenment finally betrayed itself with the technology of atrocity. If tragic nobility is no longer possible, Pinter puts his audience through an altogether different experience.

In *The Caretaker* an emotional rhythm of laughter and silence eventually creates a structure of feeling developing from the initial audience predisposition to respond to Davies as a comic tramp. His claim "I've had dinner with the best" (7) is so farcically improbable that in uproarious laughter at something so characteristic the audience hardly notices how Davies's claims offer a burlesque of their own middle-class values. Instead, the audience relishes a comic performance. As the play develops, however, and the social deprivation of Davies becomes more and more apparent, the audience is sidetracked by Davies's unremitting opportunism and nastiness and encouraged by Mick to join his side in comically baiting the tramp. The sense of game holds the ultimately serious in check by the relief of straight music hall cross-talk:

MICK: That's my bed.
DAVIES: What about that, then?
MICK: That's my mother's bed.
DAVIES: Well she wasn't in it last night!

(33)

Davies is inevitably seen as much, if not more, a victim of circumstance than of his own limitations. As a consequence, a moral sense intervenes, and laughter can be checked, but Pinter continues with great deliberation strongly counterpointing the serious and the comic, and we find both Mick's mockery ("You must come up and have a drink sometime. Listen to some Tchaikovsky" [62]) and the pure comedy of Davies ("The only way to keep a pair of shoes on, if you haven't got no laces, is to tighten the foot, see?" [63]). But Davies's earlier question, "What about me?" (59), has a troubling, poignant resonance, because it challenges conflicting impulses of charity and contempt. And it is this that fills the "*long silence*" at the close. Here Davies is no longer a comic butt, and he certainly isn't a tragic figure. Thus, unmitigated compassion does not arise, sentimentality is too simple, and pathos is too tempered by mixed responses, as the audience and Davies confront each other both as part of a performance and as part of society—united yet divided. Pinter's great achievement is in his triumph over genre and convention in art and over class and prejudice in society. Stark and ineluctable Davies remains there, an existence dramatized with an unprecedented authenticity. Pinter does not provide a neat moral resolution. Each member of an audience must make up his or her own mind. *The Caretaker* finally presents something as compelling as Father Zossima's words in Dostoevsky's *The Brothers*

Karamazov: "All are responsible for all"; or in Pinter's terms, all must care for all.

Revue Sketches

In the same year that Pinter wrote *A Night Out* and *The Caretaker* he composed several little revue sketches. The revue is a late-nineteenth-century stage form comprising heterogeneous materials of dance, song, mime, and the sketch, often of a satirical or topical nature. In an early study of postwar English drama John Russell Taylor paid brief attention to these works but prefaced his comment with the remark, "These sketches are, or course, very slight and of quite minor importance."[8] Thereafter most critics have ignored these pieces. Of fundamental importance in understanding much of Pinter's work, these sketches are practice pieces for the greater achievements. As an artist prepares for a major work by preparing sketches of parts of the whole, so some of these revue sketches have this function in relation to *The Caretaker,* particularly. The revue sketches were written for the stage revues *One to Another* ("The Black and White," "Trouble in the Works") and *Pieces of Eight* ("Last to Go," "Request Stop," "Special Offer"). Although they were written at this time, further sketches were eventually broadcast in 1964 on the BBC's *Third Program* ("That's Your Trouble," "That's All," "Applicant," "Interview," "Dialogue for Three").

The importance of these sketches was stressed in a very early *London Times* article, when Pinter insisted that he saw himself as "a dramatist some of whose work just happens to fit into the framework of a revue": "As far as I'm concerned there is no real difference between my sketches and my plays. In both I am interested primarily in people. I want to present living people to the audience, worthy of their interest basically because they *are,* they exist, not because of any moral the author might draw from them."[9] Sketches in stage revue, television, and radio shows provide comic entertainment by drawing on certain situations and commonly using the punch line formula. Situations characterizing the genre usually draw on domestic or public milieu like that of the railway station waiting room, shop, café, office, sitting room, or kitchen. A frequently found example is what might be called the newspaper sketch, in which two characters either insist on or resist interruption while reading a paper, often quoting the bizarre or being misunderstood, all for comic ends. *The Room, The Dumb Waiter, The Birthday Party, A Slight Ache,* and *The Homecoming* all begin like a newspaper sketch (as, indeed, do John Osborne's *Look Back in Anger* [1956] and N. F. Simpson's *A Resounding Tinkle* [1957]) and establish a generic humor at the outset from which the full play develops with a counterbalancing seriousness.

In Pinter's application the newspaper sketch situation is always found to have a larger dramatic function. Bert's silent engrossment in *The Room* is indicative of the relative insignificance of the completely ignored Rose. Edward's study of the high Tory *Daily Telegraph,* which opens *A Slight Ache,* is disrupted by the importunate Flora and begins the dichotomy between society and nature, public and private, which patterns the play. Max interrupts Lennie's study of the racing page in *The Homecoming* and inaugurates a whole series of polarities with domesticity and animality: Lenny fancies "Second Wind for the three-thirty," but it is Max who claims the experienced "gift" of telling "a good filly . . . a stayer" (18). He confronts Ruth later, and, indeed, she "stays." Perhaps the beginning of *The Birthday Party* is closest to the revue sketch conventions. But in Pinter's careful circular patterning we see that Meg and Petey substitute "nice bits . . . something good" (4) from public events for private uneventfulness, while McCann's tearing the newspaper into strips symbolizes the alternative intrusion of threat and violence, which Petey and Meg refuse to accept as they finally return to their newspaper. An example from the sketches may be considered, "The Black and the White." This has added interest since it was originally one of the ten prose pieces Pinter has published.

"Kullus" and "The Examinination" have been mentioned. "Mac" and "Arthur Wellard" record Pinter's memory of Anew McMaster and the old England cricketer who for a time played in Pinter's own amateur team "the Gaieties." Both pieces are brilliantly evocative and spring into life with snatches of remembered speech. "Hutton and the Past" testifies further to Pinter's devotion to cricket. "Lola," "The Coast," and "Problem" are reminiscent of *The Basement, Landscape,* and *The Collection,* respectively. But "The Black and White" and "Tea Party" have a particular interest as sources for conversion to drama. Reflecting on the all-night patrons of places like the Black and White milk bars of London, Pinter remarked: "In those cafés you find these curious night wanderers who don't seem to be going anywhere or doing anything, though obviously they must have some interest in the future, even if it only keeps them going from moment to moment—till the next bus goes by or the last paper is sold. They seemed to me extraordinarily solitary, unable to communicate with each other or anyone else, and often not even wanting to."[10] The following quotations will bring out the difference between the prose and sketch dialogue:

> Now and again you can see the all-night buses going down. They all run down there. I've never been the other way, not the way some of them go. I've been down to Liverpool Street. That's where some of them end up. She's greyer than me.[11]

(In the following section FIRST refers to "First old woman," SECOND to "Second old woman.")
First: That's another all-night bus gone down. (*Pause.*) Going up the other way. Fulham way. (*Pause.*) That was a two-nine-seven. (*Pause.*) I've never been up that way. (*Pause.*) I've been down to Liverpool Street.
SECOND: That's up the other way.
FIRST: I don't fancy going down there, down Fulham way, and all up there.
SECOND: Uh-uh.
FIRST: I've never fancied that direction much.
Pause.
SECOND: How's your bread?
FIRST: Eh?
SECOND: Your bread.
FIRST: All right. How's yours?[12]

The prose passage has all the problems associated with interior monologue, or stream-of-consciousness technique. The sense of psychological naturalism is considerably qualified by the reader's awareness of the literary approximation that has taken place. To record or evoke actual stream of consciousness is an impossibility, since an ordering artistic consciousness must supervene. As a consequence, the relative artifice of fabrication can subvert the authenticity it is striving for, depending on the skill of the writer. The sketch provides something quite different. Whereas the first strives toward the workings of the mind, the psychology of the speaker, the second is more modest—it is not about what a person thinks but, rather, how a person speaks. This is the dramatic pivot on which must turn all those questions of identity, being, communication, existence, and experience. It is this that makes examination of such minimalist works richly rewarding for understanding Pinter as a whole.

The revue sketches freed the dramatist from the mechanics of the well-made play and, in doing so, realized in epitome a kind of existential moment. This is not the case with all the sketches, some of which do indeed simply entertain. But with "The Black and White" and "Last to Go"—identified by Pinter in the *Times* interview—and "That's All," more is achieved than mere laughter. It may seem disproportionate to claim so much for such seemingly limited works, yet for Pinter they proved to be a mode he had to explore by discarding excessive symbolic baggage and thereby freeing himself from a major characteristic of the first phase of his dramatic work. In these three sketches— the exchanges between two old female tramps, between a coffee stall proprietor and an old newspaper seller, and between two housewives—being, existence, and utterance are mutually self- defining in dramatic experience. These minimalist epitomes ren- der the interdependency of being and language. Experience forms the language of habit, reflecting how lives are shaped by the naturalistic erosion of routine. In the sketches Pinter made ap- parent the fundamental impetus of all his drama—that identity is coextensive with utterance. Seemingly familiar, yet ultimately inscrutable, the characters in the sketches are socially placed by their speech in a given "world" yet have no necessary relationship with it. As Pinter noted of the cinematic opening out of the film version of *The Caretaker,* "While we go into the world outside it is almost as if only these characters exist."[13]

Names are conferred by family, society, religion, and/or nationality, but identity is shaped by life. "I never think of names at the time of writing," Pinter recorded.[14] His art here bears comparison with the Joycean epiphany. In *Stephen Hero* Joyce's character wanders around Dublin, as Pinter did around London after leaving the Royal Academy of Dramatic Art, catching at fragments of dialogue, which come to mean something to him: "This triviality made him think of collecting many such moments together in a book of epiphanies. By epiphany he meant a sudden spiritual manifestation, whether in the vulgarity of speech or of gesture or in a memorable phase of the mind itself."[15] Pinter's epiphanies, however, are less egotistic. Not self-reflexive moments in which art is a substitute for religion but, rather, a pure objective rendering of human contingency which becomes artistically absolute in its authenticity. To a considerable extent, in assaying the sketch form, Pinter realized an evident creative matrix for his work.

The Hothouse (1980)

Discussion of this lengthy two-act play, which dates from 1958, has been delayed until now since it is advantageous to approach it retrospectively, after appraising the place of the revue sketches. Originally, Pinter had adverse feelings about the work but, fortunately, locked it away rather than destroying it. Pinter felt that "it was heavily satirical and it was quite useless": "I never began to like any of the characters, they really didn't live at all. . . . The characters were so purely cardboard. I was intentionally—for the only time, I think—trying to make a point, an explicit point, that these were nasty people and I disapproved of them. And therefore they didn't begin to live."[16] Eventually, in 1979, the dramatist dug it out, laughed a lot while looking over it, and, in spite of "a certain self-indulgence in writing," such as "outpourings of wild bravura,"[17] recalling Mick in *The Caretaker,* decided that after a few cuts it would be worth producing. This was done very successfully onstage in 1980 and on television two years later. A third radical revision of Pinter's view of *The Hothouse* in the 1980s was included when he suggested political interpretations of some early plays as representing "authoritarian systems," to the extent that *The Hothouse* was actually reappraised as anticipating "how psychiatric hospitals were used particularly in Russia."[18]

Roote, the director of a mental institution, metaphorically *The Hothouse,* after possibly killing one patient and seducing another, withdraws into the seclusion of his office. The portrayal of Roote as a bureaucratic bully extends Pinter's preoccupation with power, subservience, and breakdown from the private into the public world of state institutions. A newcomer to his post, the innocent and naive young Lamb becomes, as his name anticipates, the sacrificial victim by way of electrical shock treatment, for the pregnancy of patient 6459. Otherwise, the action is largely taken up with the rivalry between Roote and his disaffected subordinates, Gibbs and Lush, as they jockey for power, of varying kinds, over one another. Gibbs finally allows the unseen patients to slaughter all the other staff.

Roote can be related to Ben (*The Dumb Waiter*), Goldberg (*The Birthday Party*), Edward (*A Slight Ache*), and later with Disson in *Tea Party* (1964). All need authorized knowledge or power, which they cannot sustain without degrees of strain, relapse, or breakdown. In many respects Roote is like a gentile version of Goldberg, in that both burlesque middle-class values, culminating, in Roote's case, with a Christmas speech consisting of a catalog of clichés as his mind seizes up. Both feel an impulse toward sentimental recall as compensation for the collapse of the present. Yet these thematic links are overturned somewhat by the relative lack of control as the play almost caves in beneath the weight of its theatricality. It is unbalanced by what Pinter came to criticize his earlier work for, those "cabaret turns"[19] in which sensationalism acts as a kind of dramatic compensation.

More generally, the formal problem with *The Hothouse* is that it is made up of largely unassimilated revue sketch materials. The interview sketch "Applicant" consists of dialogue taken from the sequence of Lamb's electric shock treatment and interrogations. Various speeches, including Roote's drunken evocation of exotic fornication, became "Dialogue for Three." *The Hothouse* opens with the boss-employee consultation format found in the sketch "Trouble in the Works." One familiar music hall routine in which an improbable description of a third party elicits comic verification was salvaged for *The Collection.* Almost throughout, in the dialogue between either Roote and Gibbs,

or Roote and Lush, can be felt the recognizable combination of
music hall comic plus straight "feed" man. Consider the following exchange:

> LUSH: I mean, not only are you a scientist, but you have literary
> ability, musical ability, knowledge of most schools of
> philosophy, philology, photography, anthropology,
> cosmology, theology, phytology, phytonomy, phytotomy—
> ROOTE: Oh, no, no, not phytotomy.

> (261)

The pseudo-learned absurdity is funny, but it is not part of
the measured contrast of laughter and seriousness as found in
something like *The Birthday Party* or *A Slight Ache*. As such, it
runs the risk of mannerism, which Pinter was well aware of, and
became an issue in *Night School,* reserved for consideration here
for this reason.

Night School (1960)

The idiom of the revue sketches in part derives from a parodic element in everyday dialogue, particularly in the unguarded
degree of repetition, which, as a consequence, can lead to the
possibility of caricature when dramatized. The three sketches
"The Black and the White," "Last to Go," and "That's All" main-
tain a fine balance, but in *Night School,* a play for television, the
control is frequently upset. For example, here is an exchange
between Millie and Annie, the relatives of Wally, who has just
returned home from prison to find that they have let his room to

Sally—apparently a schoolteacher but leading a double life as a hostess at a nightclub.

> MILLY: I don't want the milk hot, I want it cold.
> ANNIE: It is cold.
> MILLY: I thought you warmed it up.
> ANNIE: I did. The time I got up here it's gone cold.
> MILLY: You should have kept it in the pan. If you'd brought it up in the pan it would have still been hot.
> MILLY: I don't want it hot.
> ANNIE: Well, that's why I'm saying it's cold.
> MILLY: I know that. But if I had wanted it hot. That's all I'm saying. (*She sips the milk.*) It could be colder.
>
> (204)

Pinter himself has always felt qualms about this work, recognizing the danger of mannerism, initially not allowing publication, but, eventually, after a successful radio version of 1966 he included it in the collected plays. Mannerist repetition is certainly there in the details of Wally's encounter with Sally, echoing that of Stanley with Lulu and Albert with the prostitute, but there is much to be relished, particularly in the bravura creation of Mr. Solto, who undertakes to find Sally's nightclub, only to pursue her for himself, almost convincing the gullible Wally that she doesn't exist. It is as if the comic exuberance that contributed to the portrayal of Goldberg had still left creative energy in Pinter which was expended on Solto in such lines as these: "They wanted three hundred and fifty pounds income tax off me the other day. My word of honour. I said to them, you must be mad! What are you trying to do, bring me to an early death? Buy me a cheap spade I'll get up first thing in the morning before breakfast and dig my own grave" (199). As a small boy, Pinter was taken to the music hall at the Hackney Empire, where such dialogue as the following would have been entirely in place:

> SOLTO: I killed a man with my own hands, a six-foot-ten Lascar from Madagascar.
> ANNIE: From Madagascar?
> SOLTO: Sure. A Lascar.
> ANNIE: Alaska?
> SOLTO: Madagascar.

(200)

And there are shades here of Flanagan and Allen and the Crazy Gang Show, at London's postwar Victoria Palace.

Whatever the limitations of *Night School,* it certainly has aspects that make it worthy of study and add to knowledge of Pinter's work by the comparisons it offers, of Solto with Goldberg and Walter with Albert in *A Night Out.* Walter, like Albert, is impelled to psychological fantasy in the presence of a young woman. He glamorizes his status of petty forger of post office books by pretending to be the leader of an armed robbery gang. Like Albert, he bosses about the girl, who, similar to her counterpart, has seeming fantasies of gentility, as a schoolteacher.

While not fully resolved, the play does offer a fascinating contrast of social and psychological realities and fantasies. Uncomplicatedly immersed in the world of everyday are Millie and Annie. Wally's fantasies are evident, and, though some critics consider Solto to be a rich landlord masquerading as hard up, this view is not very convincing. All Solto's anecdotes indicate a congenital liar who uses the comically outrageous to mask the very ordinariness of a postwar spiv who has made a few pounds and consequently likes to think of himself as something more imposing. The nightclubs he visits and refers to would have been full of such people. More interesting is Sally. The two photographs discovered in Wally's room confirm that she is both a nightclub hostess and a schoolteacher. And in the nightclub, if the manager's claim that "she speak three languages" is accepted (215), then there is the possibility that, indeed, she has attended a night school. If this is the case, then Sally offers the complete obverse of that mundane reality of Annie and Molly—someone whose life is completely divided into acceptable and unacceptable moral realities, in which the seeming reality, a nightclub hostess, is a lived fantasy, and the seeming fantasy of education is a reality to be subverted.

From this point of view, with differing planes of reality, both social and psychological, from mundanity to prostitution and criminality, *Night School* may be considered as a precursor of *The Homecoming* (1964). It is obligatory to study a writer's oeuvre to gain a larger understanding of both individual works, and vice versa. With a great writer nothing can be said to be redundant or expendable.

The Dwarfs (1960)

Some hilarious lines in *Night School* concerning Wally's projection of himself as prospective keeper of manuscripts and plunderer of ancient tombs derive from Pinter's novel of the early 1950s, *The Dwarfs*, the title of which probably derives from the Proteus section of Joyce's *Ulysses* ("Then from the starving cagework like a horde of jerkined dwarfs, my people"), an influence deeply felt in the novel, which was not published until 1990. Much of its contents, however, were used for Pinter's play of the same title. The elliptical nature of the piece has proven to be dramatically recalcitrant, and it has rarely, if ever, been staged since 1963. This is regrettable, since the play has great value in itself and as part of Pinter's developing oeuvre. In fact, the play's concern with friendship and betrayal is central to almost all of Pinter's work and is another manifestation of his lifelong preoccupation with power in relationships. In this antisentimental view friendship consists in a due hierarchy of influence and regard, which collapses when subject to the betrayals of doubt, enmity, or mistrust. The caretaker dwarfs are fantasy creatures of the disturbed volatile mind of Len, who in turn acts as caretaker for them, all the while obliquely appealing to his friends Pete and Mark for the care he needs from them in reality.

Mark has established himself as a successful actor, while, in contrast to his bohemian and aesthetic independence, Pete has submitted to middle-class conformity and become an office worker in the city. Len is a porter at Paddington station. The different social positioning of these young Jewish Londoners with intellectual aspirations anticipates the breakup of common ground. Pinter focuses here on one of the commonest and most psychologically fraught aspects of friendship—the inadmissible perception of the disintegration of a facade that still stands, albeit on perished foundations, though ready to fall at the push of a single expression like "Pete thinks you're a fool" (100), as Len tells Mark.

With great subtlety of nuance and allusion Pinter plays off different kinds of Jewish background at this East End court of Elsinore. *Hamlet* has prominence in the novel, but in the play it figures elliptically as Len, the Hamlet-like soliloquist, believes he is being played upon by his Rosencrantz and Guildenstern, as he fingers a refractory recorder. As the smartly dressed Mark arrives, the resentful and flustered Pete, who formerly affected ignorance of Mark's particular Jewish background (Sephardic/Portuguese), asserts his own (Ashkenazi/Polish); Mark is heard inquiring, "Any tea?" and Pete's reply, "Polish tea" (84), codifies his resistance. It is this kind of subtlety which demands great concentration in Pinter's audience. To some extent this was the problem with the philosophical speeches of Len, seemingly concerned with issues of ontology and epistemology, identity and verification, yet in fact using such topics for ulterior purposes. Len cannot confront reality because he cannot yet forgo the assumed friendship of the three. One of the difficulties of the play is that the philosophical speeches of Len have been taken at face value by critics, but he is really trying to make an appeal when made desperate by the fact that he senses its impossibility, thus the self-defeating obliquity of his language. Consider the following example:

> The rooms we live in . . . open and shut. (*Pause.*) Can't you see? They change shape at their own will. I wouldn't grumble if only they would keep to some consistency. But they don't. And I can't tell the limits, the boundaries, which I've been led to believe are natural. I'm all for the natural behaviour of rooms, doors, staircases, the lot. But I can't rely on them. When, for example, I look through a train window, at night, and see the yellow lights, very clearly, I can see what they are, and I see that they're still. But they're only still because I'm moving. (87)

Len uses the guise of philosophy for what is really an analogy concerning the relationship of himself and Mark. It is Len who remains "still" domestically, while Mark "moves" as itinerant actor, emotionally and geographically distancing himself from Len. The contrast in their furniture emphasizes this—modern for Mark, older middle European for Len. Mark knows what is taking place, as, indeed, Len knows that Mark's indifference is the most damaging response of all. Pete and Mark still make gestures ("I'm supposed to be a friend of yours" [94], "You want to listen to your friends, mate" [97]), but both refuse to respond to the desperate indirect appeal Len is making throughout the play, and particularly in the calculated fantasy of the dwarfs, which is evidently a grotesque metamorphosis of his relationship with them. Manifestly, the domestic sensationalism of the dwarf figures is in inverse proportion to their own coolness and distance. Immersed in offal and filth, the dwarfs expressionistically dramatize a crucial phrase of the novel, "this abortion we called friendship" (174). Finally, banishing Pete and Mark, emblematized by the filth of the gull and the spider, and with them their alter ego dwarfs, Len is left alone, free from his intellectual vortex, to his own aseptic solitude.

Notes

1. "Harold Pinter 1991," *The Pinter Review* (1991): 65.
2. "Interview with Harold Pinter" (with Kenneth Tynan), 28 October 1960, BBC transcript, pt. 1, 8.
3. *Ibid.*

4. "A Conversation [Pause] with Harold Pinter," reprinted in *Critical Essays on Harold Pinter,* edited by Steven H. Gale (Boston: G. K. Hall, 1990) 27.

5. *Ibid.,* 23.

6. "Writing for Myself," *Plays Two,* (London: Faber, 1991), xi.

7. "Harold Pinter Replies," *New Theatre Magazine,* 2 January 1961, 8.

8. *Anger and After* (Harmondsworth: Penguin Books, 1963), 332.

9. "Mr. Harold Pinter—Avant-Garde Playwright and Intimate Review," *The Times,* 16 November 1959, 4.

10. *Ibid.*

11. *Plays One,* 377–8.

12. *Plays Two,* 229.

13. "Filming *The Caretaker*" (Harold Pinter and Clive Donner interviewed by Kenneth Cavander), *Transatlantic Review* 13, (1963): 23.

14. "A Play and Its Politics. A Conversation between Harold Pinter and Nicholas Hern," preface to *One for the Road* (London: Methuen, 1984), 15.

15. London: Cape, 1956, 216. For a fuller consideration of the revue sketches see Ronald Knowles, "*The Hothouse* and the Epiphany of Harold Pinter," *Journal of Beckett Studies* 10 (1985).

16. "Harold Pinter: An Interview" (with Lawrence Bensky), in *Pinter: A Collection of Critical Essays,* edited by Arthur Ganz (Englewood Cliffs, N.J.: Prentice-Hall, 1972), 28.

17. *The New York Times,* 30 December 1979, 7.

18. *Omnibus,* BBC 1, 21 October 1988. See chapter 8 below.

19. "Interview with Harold Pinter" (with Kenneth Tynan), 28 October 1960, BBC transcript, pt. 1, 8.

CHAPTER FOUR

Television Plays and Screenplays of the 1960s

The televisual techniques that might have saved *The Dwarfs* were developed in the four main plays for the small screen in the 1960s. All four plays show Pinter's developing mastery of the medium, and to some extent that mastery developed in reaction to the "failure" of *The Dwarfs*. Pinter's range was matched by the all-important cutting and fluidity of camera work. What might seem cumbersome and distracting in split, triple staging, as in *The Dwarfs,* is perfectly natural on-screen. Pinter's technical accomplishment is fully achieved in the experimentalism of *The Basement* (1966, broadcast 1967). Yet, as if aware of the seductive freedom of the camera, Pinter reacted by seeking tighter formal controls in parallelism, permutation, and complementarity.

The Collection (1961)

A Slight Ache introduced the issue of marital betrayal in Pinter's drama, but in terms of the menace of a symbolic intruder, whereas, in the naturalistic mode of *The Collection* (1961),

77

betrayal occupies the whole drama and remains substantially central in Pinter's work up to *Betrayal* (1978) itself. *The Collection* takes advantage of a form that permeates many nineteenth- and twentieth-century genres, preeminently the mystery, the thriller, and the detective story. That is, the plot turns on the problem of verification, in which there are several versions of the same events or situation. Among the most celebrated examples of this in twentieth century art are Pirandello's play *Right You Are (If You Think So)* (1917) and Kurosawa's film *Rashomon* (1950). Pinter, however, brings to a latter-day comedy of Belgravia-Chelsea manners an implicit depth of his own, as it is finally realized that the "truth" pursued actually masks a deeper and more painful reality.

In the elegant Belgravia house Bill shares with Harry, James confronts the former with his wife's, Stella's, account of an affair in Leeds while showing a dress collection. Although Bill adds seemingly provocative details, he eventually gives his own version—only a brief flirtation, with kissing, took place. Reciprocally, Harry faces Stella, who claims that the story is Bill's invention, which Harry repeats to James and Bill but claiming that Stella made up the story. Finally, Bill revises his version, announcing that the truth was that he and Stella did nothing but merely talked about sex. In the final shot Stella looks at James "*neither confirming nor denying*" (145) this version of events. The enigma, however, is not what really took place in Leeds but, rather, what is really taking place in James's mind as he seeks one "truth" in order to evade another.

As Pinter found with the film of *The Caretaker*, in the smile of the two brothers, camera close-up could suggestively bring out the metalanguage of body and face, gesture and expression, which reinforces subtextual depth. Consequently, the combination of minimal chitchat, pauses, and facial close-ups creates an unspoken doubt about what the precise state of the relationship is between the two couples, Stella and James and Harry and Bill. Consider the following exchanges:

> STELLA: I'm going.
> *Pause.*
> Aren't you coming in today?
> *Pause.*
> JAMES: No.
> STELLA: You had to meet those people from . . .
> *Pause. She slowly walks to an armchair, picks up her jacket and puts it on.*
> You had to meet those people about that order.
>
> (110)

> HARRY: You didn't make any toast this morning.
> BILL: No. Do you want some?
> HARRY: No. I don't.
> BILL: I can if you like.
> HARRY: It's all right. Don't bother.
>
> (112)

Since they never directly confront the issue, the audience assumes that they are not themselves sufficiently in possession of facts or aware of feelings to know either between themselves or to themselves individually what the situation is. Bill gives voice to the enigma at the heart of the play: "Surely the wound heals when you know the truth, doesn't it? I mean, when the truth is verified?" (139). Unfortunately, the truths of human psychology are not always such as to be readily available for objective verification.

Unable to face the truth in himself, James represents his charade of friendship with Bill as the rediscovery of a boyish companionship, though in fact it varies from almost "rough trade" threat of brutality to mildly homosexual flirtatiousness. As such, he reenacts the betrayal he insists on, yet the homosexual burlesque reveals his own lack of conviction. It appears that James resorts to strategies of boyhood because he can't really face the adult complexities of either homosexuality or heterosexuality. The human realities of friendship and betrayal will be brought into a sharper perspective when *Betrayal* is considered in terms of the theoretical approach of gender studies. With James, in *The Collection,* and Edward, in *A Slight Ache,* is introduced a psychological and dramatic complex that came to dominate Pinter's writing: the pain of the rejected male.

It appears that James seeks evidence of conventional adultery because he cannot face whatever the real reasons are for the breakdown of his marriage, which seems to have been taking place before any visit to Leeds. Bill recognizes an obsessiveness in James's story which cannot be expunged, so he plays along with it, giving vent to a latent bisexuality by which he reciprocally recognizes the breakdown of his relationship with Harry. Stella's story is a half-truth. Evasively, James created a vivid fiction from whatever detail he persuaded her to relate or invent. Harry turns the story around because he does not wish to provoke James any further and thus endanger his own relationship, but Bill's final account, seemingly a revision of the truth between himself and Stella, in fact signals the end of his relationship with Harry. By revealing Stella's collusion, Bill forces James back to the harsher truth of prior disaffection—but James clings to the treadmill of necessary doubt:

> You just sat and talked about what you would do if you went to your room. That's what you did.
> *Pause.*
> Didn't you?
> *Pause.*
> That's the truth . . . isn't it? (145)

The Lover (1963)

As Pirandello is often mentioned in the context of *The Collection,* so Jean Genet is frequently referred to in discussion of *The Lover*—that is, Genet of *The Maids* (1953), which is concerned with role-playing and power-subservience relationships. In this consideration of Pinter as a television dramatist it is important to note that the currently available text reprints that of 1964, which was a text for the Arts Theatre production, whereas the first, 1963 edition, included screen directions for the original television presentation. In fact, there are hardly any differences in dialogue between the two, but Pinter's screen directions at the outset create a specific emphasis. Of minor importance is the visual swap of the city financier's, Richard's, Eton tie (TV) for a bowler hat (stage). Clearly, the stage needed a more pronounced social signal than a diagonal stripe. Of major importance in the television production, however, was the sexually emphatic symbolism of the bongo drums used in the erotic role-playing games of Richard and his wife, Sarah, behind the blinds in their Windsor seclusion and an extensive wordless sequence involving Sarah's cosmetic preparations.

Joan Kemp-Welch's direction of the black and white production, which won a "play of the year" accolade, begins with one of the most celebrated openings in British television drama of the 1960s. After the title, the actors' names, and frozen silhouettes of the characters in frantic postures, Kemp-Welch graphically realized Pinter's opening directions for the small screen. In a protracted sequence focusing on another silhouette of the bongo drum, fingers and hands are seen tapping, stroking, interlocking, grappling, and coupling, like a pair of orgasmic tarantulas on its surface, to the increasingly intense striking of the drum. Thereafter, the bongo drum is included in other shots and, reciprocally, concludes the play.

Almost immediately, following the brief opening exchanges, between the consecutive "*Lights fade*" and "*Fade up*" of the 1964 stage text, after Richard's first departure, a full four-minute sequence takes place, without any dialogue, of erotic body close-ups of Sarah's preparations—stockings, garter, zippers, the tight, showy dress lovingly patted. Then the camera focuses on Sarah's face as she moves to her dressing table, where she applies perfume, inspects jewelry, checks her coiffure. The erotic and the narcissistic are both heavily emphasized by the camera's dwelling on mirrors. The sequence continues downstairs with high-heeled shoes, further pampering, and mirrors, until the doorbell sounds, and a male figure seen from behind is coyly admitted by Sarah.

These differences from the current text at the outset contributed provocatively to the erotic element, emphasizing the carnal end of all the games. Presumably, it was this that contributed
to the view of the general manager of the television company
that *The Lover* should only be watched by married people and
was quite unsuitable for the unmarried below the age of twenty-
three.

The Lover has attracted varied critical comment, since the
nature of its concerns are germane to many fields of contemporary theoretical study, particularly that of feminism and psychoanalysis. A common view tends to take the line that the play is
about the struggle to unify love and desire, sex and marriage,
social and sexual identity. Yet the 1963 production really brought
out power-subservience in the Genet-like core of the play. An
initial difficulty is that several critics fail to recognize that the
sexual games played by Richard as "Max" and Sarah as "Dolores/
Mary" are on Sarah's terms, not Richard's. In their role-playing
sex fantasies they both play, alternatively, various scenes of se-
ducer and innocent. But the first erotic sequence derives from
Sarah's wishes, even when she affects to be demure and innocent. Richard begins to undermine this long-standing erotic ar-
rangement by inquiring, "Does it ever occur to you that while
you're spending the afternoon being unfaithful to me I'm sitting
at a desk going through balance sheets and graphs?" This could
all be alternative role-playing, but Sarah's answers indicate otherwise: "What a funny question. . . . You've never asked me that
before" (153).

Then, having mistakenly failed to change back from part of
her fantasy game erotica, Sarah is told by Richard that he does
not keep a mistress but, instead, a "whore" (155), clearly signal-

ing his dissatisfaction with the status quo. This impels Sarah to question this newly revealed relationship, as Richard had just earlier began to question the established practice: "You don't normally do that" (159), Sarah comments—"Asking me so many questions about . . . my side of it" (158–59). As Sarah has forgotten to change out of her stiletto-heeled shoes, so Richard proceeds to deliberately break one of the fundamental rules of the game, that Richard and "Max" must be kept apart, or at least one must not encroach on the other. "Why does he put up with it?" (168), "Max" asks, a question taking an unprecedented direction as Sarah points out, but "Max" protests further that he can't go on deceiving his wife! For a moment Sarah begins losing the situation—"I wish you'd stop this rubbish, anyway. . . . You're doing your best to ruin the whole afternoon" (170)—and attempts to recover old ground, but "Max" insists, "I've played my last game" (171), and rejects Sarah as "too bony" (172).

Richard then returns to criticize his wife's "debauchery" (177) and introduces the bongo drum as evidence, insisting that Sarah reveal its illicit function. In the television production the camera moved into close-up, picking up Sarah's increasing disorientation, until finally she is made to comply by collusion with Richard's sexual strategy to install her as his "whore." Sarah agrees to change her clothes, thereby realizing his fantasies, becoming his "lovely whore" (184), as the symbolic bongo drum sequence had suggested at the outset by having the male hand entrap and turn the female hand upside down. Far from unifying love and desire, Richard's strategy brings the situation balanced by parity of exchange in roles to one of polarity, Sarah becoming respectable wife and disrespectable whore—another anticipation, to a certain extent, of *The Homecoming.*

TELEVISION PLAYS AND SCREENPLAYS OF THE 1960s

The Basement (1967)

The Collection exploited the technique of quick cutting to emphasize parallelism (with the witty inverted dramatic irony that Bill and Stella never actually face each other), while *The Lover* exploited a wordless visual sequence. In *The Basement* and *Tea Party* Pinter developed greater versatility in the visual medium in writing for television and at the same time began his distinguished career as a writer of screenplays. *The Basement* was written to join a trio of films along with two by Ionesco and Beckett. Beckett wrote *Film* (1963), but Ionesco's contribution was never completed, and, as a consequence, *The Basement* was not broadcast until 1967. In narrative terms the plot reexamines sexual and territorial imperatives that have appeared before in Pinter's work. Stott and Jane arrive at Law's basement flat and seemingly displace him, while a complicated, vacillatory love triangle develops, culminating in a fight for possession of space and sex. What is quite different in this work, however, is the subordination of the verbal to the visual. The fundamental theatrical elements of a fixed stage and the necessity of voice projection are determinants no longer, and Pinter allows his imagination a fluidity and freedom to match the visual medium.

The printed text of *The Basement* consists, in fact, of a roughly equal proportion of dialogue to camera directions and set details. Without actually seeing the original production, it calls for a particularly active and vivid imagination to follow through the visual revolutions within the total circularity of the play. Turning from the limits of naturalism, Pinter explores the fluidity of the camera to find expressive form in which social and psychological rivalry in friendship, love, and possession can be reflected. Reality, space, and time take on this fluidity, as youthful wishful thinking moves from oral imposture to objective reality, and vice versa.

Law welcomes Stott into his comfortable, though modest, basement flat. Stott is without a car, is soaking wet, and seems to be without anywhere to stay. Law twice reminds Stott of their modest origins—"That awful place in Chatsworth Road" (148). If friendship, from one point of view, inevitably entails rivalry, then Law seems a winner and Stott a loser. But the lonely Law only has a Persian love manual, while Stott has a beautiful young girlfriend of flesh and blood, who is eventually introduced into the basement and immediately strips with Stott and begins to make love, while Law returns to his printed erotica. The unrealistic alacrity of the unselfconscious lovers suggests a psychological projection of Law's fear of rivalry and longing for love.

From this point "action" is largely replaced by alternating shots: between exterior and interior, between winter and summer, between day and night, and between the alternating decor of Law's flat. To collapse all this into a mere dream of Law's as he nods off by the fire would be to diminish the expressionistic subtleties that the work has. Excluding the opening and closing circularity of the exterior of the basement entrance, there are approximately forty shots roughly divided between exterior and interior. A focal image repeated twice is that of Stott and Jane in bed. Unifying all the rest is the developing pattern of rivalry for Jane's sexual allegiance and for possession of the room signalized by aesthetic preferences. Stott initially criticizes the lighting, persuades Law to reject his watercolors, and, most striking of all, the basement is twice transformed by complete replace-

ment of furnishings. Here are Pinter's directions for the two trans-
formations: *"The room is unrecognizable. The furnishing has
changed. There are Scandinavian tables and desks. Large bowls
of Swedish glass. Tubular chairs. An Indian rug. Parquet floors,
shining. A new hi-fi cabinet, etc."* (153); *"The room is unrecognizable. The walls are hung with tapestries, an oval Florentine
mirror, an oblong Italian Master. The floor is marble tiles. There
are marble pillars with hanging plants, carved golden chairs, a
rich carpet along the room's centre"* (159).

The modish Scandinavian and antique Italian palazzo sets
realize the dreams of fashion, elegance, and wealth of the past,
the alternative extreme to Chatsworth Road, complementing
Law's fantasy of Stott, his "First in Sanskrit at Oxford," his "three
chateaux," his "Facel Vega" (150). The acquirements of culture,
however, are measured by primitive aggression, as the men,
against a now bare set, clash with broken bottles, Jane making
coffee in the background, all against the high culture lyricism of
Debussy's "Girl with the Flaxen Hair" (163). The intercut shots
eliminate narrative cause to emphasize primal condition beneath
the social veneer, and, correspondingly, in the closing shots roles
and dialogue are precisely reversed, Law and Jane entering Stott's
basement, suggesting the truer common drives of masculine in-
stinct and impulse, rather than that of individual identity.

Tea Party (1965)

This play was commissioned by the European Broadcasting Union and was shown by all sixteen member countries, styled
together as "The Largest Theater in the World." Here the self-

made owner of a sanitary engineering company, Disson, can be related closely to Roote in *The Hothouse.* Both provide studies of autocratic emptiness, bluster, and breakdown, aspects of which were introduced with Goldberg (*The Birthday Party*) and Edward (*A Slight Ache*). Again, Pinter was drawn to the symbolism of blindness, but here it is closely integrated with the medium of television.

At the same time as he takes on a new secretary, Wendy, who has left her old job because of her employer's sexual harassment, Disson marries into the upper classes and employs his new brother-in-law, Willy. Thereafter, Disson believes that, just as he is drawn by Wendy's provocative body language, he is also witnessing his displacement and betrayal in the office, at home, and in bed, by Willy. But does Disson actually see what really takes place, or is what appears from his point of view no more than paranoid delusions? Unlike the visual technique of *The Basement,* which quickly moves into interchanging planes of reality and fantasy, at the beginning of *Tea Party* the solid business world of office, staff, and products is invoked. It is true that revue sketch possibilities are hinted at in the boss-interviewee format, with Disson speaking like a dictating machine, but, as always in Pinter, there are serious undertones beneath the comic surface.

At first Disson is the commanding, managerial bureaucrat, but his self-doubt becomes apparent on his honeymoon: "I make you happy, don't I? Happier than you've ever been . . . with any other man" (102). Domestically, his two children by a previous wife seem to defer to their new uncle Willy, rather than to their father's authority. As the upper-class superiority of Diana and

Willy seems to undermine Disson's potency, so he in turn exploits his power in the office by touching Wendy's body. Disson's insecurities arise in part from the irreconcilability of the simplistic business ethic he imposes on all spheres of life with the reality of his own moral vagaries when provoked by Wendy's sensuality: "I don't like self-doubt. I don't like fuzziness. I like clarity. Clear intention. Precise execution. Black or White?" (105). Disson's question concerning coffee ironically reflects his cut-and-dried view of the world, and this moral astigmatism is given visual expression by means of his erratic eyesight.

At first Disson sees double, the phallic Willy seemingly serving two balls in a game of Ping-Pong—presumably Pinter's burlesque of a Freudian castration complex. Then he resorts to the protective comfort of Wendy's chiffon scarf for his sore eyes, but nevertheless the visual encroaches: "*Suddenly* WENDY's *body appears in enormous close-up. Her buttocks fill the screen*" (121). Finally, Disson appears at an anniversary tea party with his eyes bandaged by his optician. Camera shots in sequence are from "DISSON's *point of view.*" Since he cannot actually see, what appears on the television screen is either taking place or is a projection of Disson's delusions of betrayal, conspiracy, and incest:

> WILLY *puts one arm round* WENDY, *the other round* DIANA.
> *He leads them to* WENDY's *desk.*
> WILLY *places cushions on the desk.*
> DIANA *and* WENDY, *giggling silently, hoist themselves up onto the desk. They lie head to toe.* (137)

As indicated here, no dialogue is heard during these shots. Since the bizarre actions seem unlikely at such a public event, does the visual indicate, alternatively, Disson's insight into an unsavory reality both outside and within him? With one small detail Pinter leaves the question open. When the optician removes the bandages after Disson falls, his *"eyes are open"* (138). An emphasis repeated shortly after, at the close: "DISSON's *face in close-up.* DISSON's *eyes. Open"* (40). Closed eyes would have implied complete self-delusion; open eyes suggest otherwise.

The Servant (1963)

Joseph Losey, the film director, came to Britain after the war as a refugee from the Communist investigations of the McCarthy era in the United States. He found the British class system overwhelming and all-pervasive, so much so that few, he felt, were free from its pressure. Perhaps not surprisingly, Losey was deeply affected by *A Night Out* and wrote to Pinter recording his response: "How impressed and moved I was by your play. . . . It has an intensity and inner truth both horrifying and purgative. There are few things, if any, I have seen on British TV that can compare with it."[1] In adapting Robin Maugham's 1948 novel, *The Servant,* Pinter and Losey directly confronted aspects of postwar class consciousness in the subject matter but added a psychological depth. Obviously, Maugham's original work has to be acknowledged, but Pinter took so little from the short, fifty-page novella, in fact, that *The Servant* screenplay deserves to be considered as virtually Pinter's own creation and part of his developing oeuvre.

The story concerns Tony, an upper-class capitalist entrepreneur manqué, and his newly employed manservant, Barrett, who eventually destroys him by creating a total dependence—social, psychological, and sexual. Apart from the general situation Pinter only took two substantial scenes from the book: Tony's first sexual overture with Vera, Barrett's fiancée masquerading as his sister, and Tony's unexpected return to his home late at night and confrontation with the servants, who are using his bedroom for sexual excitement. Of necessity, Maugham's intensively romantic narrator is dropped, and his almost Gothic Barrett is completely changed. The whole scene is updated from the immediately postwar period, with its former officer and black market ambience, to the then contemporary world of 1960s Chelsea.

Tony and Barrett against such a backdrop seemed to be anachronisms. Barrett's appearance—provincial, extremely staid, and conservative—made him somewhat anomalous in that fashionable setting, and the ever-self-indulgent Tony is first discovered in an after-lunch doze swathed in the military-style overcoat by which former officers signaled their caste. In contrast again, Barrett's Manchester accent evokes the industrial Midlands, while Tony's upper-class speech and proprietorial manner indicate the opposite, those born to metropolitan affluence and all that it denotes. Although the film is shot in an entirely realistic mode, these polarities are so overt that they serve as a semiotic projection that promotes an almost allegorical significance greater than simple narrative.

Once again Pinter is drawn to power-subservience relationships, an intruder taking over territory, and sexual rivalry, but here with a more pronounced class emphasis than anything before. In David Caute's words: "[Losey] at long last . . . had a screenplay unspoilt by stock studio formulas, melodrama and tedious exposition. For the first time a writer offered him the primacy of the implicit over the explicit, with human conflict percolating through the masking tape of received language, idiom and gesture."[2]

Putting together the sedulous detail Pinter provides, it appears that Tony is a descendant of the rentier-capitalist aristocracy, just returned from Africa. Many of the furnishings he crams into his newly acquired house obviously descended from more palatial circumstances. His late father was a friend of Lord Barr, and Tony and his fiancée visit the country seat of family friends, Lord and Lady Mountset. Tony's precise financial situation is never made plain. He drives a Mercedes sports car and sets himself up as an urban aristocrat, though at one point he seems to let slip that his funds can only support a provisional independence: "I can manage for a good few months" (13), he says. So it would appear that his dabbling in enterprise capitalism, the construction of whole cities in Brazil, is to enable him to continue enjoying the aristocratic lifestyle he is bent on perpetuating with his manservant.

Yet the Brazilian venture seems more a fantasy than a reality and is made to seem less and less credible as the film proceeds. (Although it is never stated, it is as if Tony were the unknowing victim of an outrageous con trick.) This comes out particularly in the strongly satirical scenes at Lord Mountset's estate, which Pinter added to the original novella. But, as always with Pinter, the seemingly inconsequential or humorous is seen to have a point.

SUSAN: Oh but some of the jungle will have to be cleared,
    won't it?
TONY: Some of the jungle, yes. A little bit.
LADY MOUNTSET: That's where the Ponchos are, of course, on
    the plains.
SUSAN: Ponchos?
LORD MOUNTSET: South American cowboys.
SUSAN: Are they called Ponchos?
LORD MOUNTSET: They were in my day.

(25)

In a house that seems more like a mausoleum than a home,
Lord and Lady Mountset almost pose like country house exhib-
its quibbling over the definition of a Brazilian "poncho," all the
while meaning "gaucho." Their speech, their house, and their
class are all made to seem anachronistic and comically redundant. But there is greater point to the satire here: capitalist and
colonialist exploitation of cultures for material profit quite igno-
rant of, and indifferent to, the character of the people concerned
is ironically reflected in Tony's seignorial proprietorship over
his very own Mancunian native.

However, Barrett is no Lawrentian primitive. As a self-pro-
claimed "gentleman's gentleman" (49), he shows himself to be
a master of interior decor, a wine connoisseur, and a gourmet,
but his dedication to upper-class values of politeness, taste, and
discrimination are hypocritical. Initially, with Tony he is self-
effacing, compliant, and deferential, while in scenes with others, including Vera, who he has promoted as maid, he is vulgar,
crude, and bumptious. With Tony's increasing dependence on
alcohol and Vera's sexual favors, the upper-class values he seems

to represent are shown to be as superficial as Barrett's. As his servant fulfills various roles, so Tony's dependence and ultimate degradation are seen to derive not so much from himself or Barrett as individuals but, rather, from a decadent class system. Barrett acts as mother, nanny, nurse, and friend and as a surrogate wife, lover, and boyfriend. And here the social reflects the psychological. Barrett needs a proxy father in "the master." When this role is in abeyance or absent, Barrett and Vera start acting like naughty children while "father" is away. Conversely, as "equals," Barrett and Tony revert to childlike games. Finally, in an alcoholic stupor amid the miasma of Chelsea whores at a party, "Tone" is imprisoned behind the elegant stair rail, with Barrett as his exploitative jailer.

The Pumpkin Eater (1964)

Discussion of Jack Clayton's film version of Penelope Mortimer's novel of 1962 most commonly considers such issues as the problem of a subjective first-person narrative and an objective camera; the seeming lack of causation for the breakdown of Jo, the central figure; and, in spite of prizewinning awards, the relative failure of the work compared to Pinter's screenplays before and after. On the contrary, *The Pumpkin Eater* is a very fine feminist film, before its time, which has gone generally unrecognized, and Pinter's real contribution has been unacknowledged. Feminism seeks recognition of the way a society largely shaped by the male also shapes women and covertly promotes this construction in the ideological use of art and the media.

The Pumpkin Eater centers on the nervous breakdown of
Jo, events both immediate and distant leading up to it, and its
aftermath. Jo is a sexually passionate woman of deep maternal
feelings, who, consequently, has married several times and has a
large brood of approximately eight children by the end of the
film. Jo fulfills, and enjoys fulfilling, the role of lover and mother.
But there is a very powerful irony here, since, whereas today a
feminist depiction would commonly portray a woman in revolt
against such a position (for example, Willy Russell's *Shirley
Valentine* and *Educating Rita*), Jo only seeks the mutuality of
her husband to sustain her role as wife.

The action of the film reveals the instability of the very function a patriarchal society insists on. Jake, Jo's current husband,
has great success in fathering his own child, becoming wealthy
in his screenwriting career, and philandering both casually and
earnestly as the opportunity arises. Jo is faithful; Jake repeatedly betrays her while insisting on his love—therefore, she is
denied the role she has accepted. As her family expands, so it
becomes the only role she has left, but this is taken away from
her as the maternal gives way to the managerial, a well-off
middle-class life providing nannies and boarding schools. As
wealth increases and possessions—houses, consumer goods—
accrue accordingly, so the role of motherhood is occluded, pre-
figuring what would happen anyway with later middle age. This
is obliquely indicated in the film's inclusion of the death scenes
of her father and father-in-law, leaving their wives with the one
final female role of lonely widowhood. Conversely, with great
understated subtlety, Jo's two elder boys return from boarding
school for the funerals, adolescent and estranged, left to the de-
termining compensations of public school masculinity.

Wherever she turns Jo is confronted with the masculine power structure of her husband's crass business associates, doctors, surgeons, and psychiatrists, all of whom are concerned in one way or another with the function of the body, not with what has happened to her mind. The literal and symbolic outcome is an abortion and hysterectomy, leaving her sterile and available for sex. This leads to the most famous scene of the film and, indeed, one of the most famous scenes of 1960s British cinema— her breakdown in Harrods, the famous West End department store, "of all places" (83), as Jake remarks, the measure of his sympathy and understanding.

Jo's isolation before her breakdown is portrayed in several ways. Immediacy of confrontation is denied by her constantly being seen behind windows and curtains. Now well-off, she becomes the bearer of fashion, a mannequin whose function is as an accessory to the expensive aesthetic and efficient objects that make a pseudo-home, in marked contrast to the makeshift barn in which she lived with an earlier husband. The broad-brimmed stylish hat turns to occlude her as she becomes no more than a model, like the sculpted heads glimpsed in her house—and as the deportment of the actress, Anne Bancroft, emphasized.

Wandering through Harrods, from department to department, sharing Jo's point of view, the audience sees all the objects that go to make up comfortable and gracious middle-class life, and for Jo it is entirely empty and meaningless—thus, the significance of the shots of her isolated in the empty new house as she removes a hat and earrings by a window. Jo breaks down, tears streaming, because she is caught between the contradictions of a male-ordered society. The doctor feels that she, as an attractive woman, should continue with childbearing; the surgeon later counsels the reverse. Her husband continually uses emotional blackmail to imply that his position as provider and responsible stepparent should exonerate his adultery. A friend decries Jake's adultery with his wife yet attempts the same thing, unsuccessfully, with Jo.

Some small scenes reveal to Jo her position. For example, a woman in the hairdresser's has been driven half-crazy by her fear of being undesirable following a hysterectomy. Jo realizes the truth of her language later ("my life is an empty place" [91]). A gently crazed, elderly West Indian caller announces himself "the new King of Israel," avowing that unhappiness derives from "the gift of love" being given to "unworthy men and unworthy women" (126). Both marginalized figures are unbalanced: one curses; the other blesses. Again, Jo is caught in the middle. Her symbolic refuge lies in facing the emptiness of the new house.

But here Jo is entrapped by sex, gender, and society as well as her own psychology. Staring from the window, she hears, then sees, her family climbing the brow of the hill: *"fanning out like trappers, converging on house"* (134) is Pinter's revealing camera direction. As they invade the house with noise and food, Jo cannot escape their united expectations. The camera work is crucial here. Going from Jake's face to Jo's, complex thoughts, feelings, and apprehensions are signaled. Jake's chummy smile, with deliberate naivete, oblivious to his own insidious shallowness, in part masks his habitual unconscious blackmail in using the children. Jo's generosity of spirit, her love and responsibility, complies with the symbolism of circular, all-encompassing domesticity. But just before the credits her smile is troubled, the light darkens, and she looks slightly down with the final image of tear-stained apprehension—an image that recalls the epigraph for the novel:

> Peter, Peter, Pumpkin eater,
> Had a wife and couldn't keep her.
> He put her in a pumpkin shell
> And there he kept her very well.

The Quiller Memorandum (1966)

With the screenplay for *The Quiller Memorandum* (1966), from Adam Hall's spy thriller, Pinter returned to the postwar world of the cold war, with the Berlin location of recrudescent nazism. Pinter's restraint simplified the narrative of the novel and expunged much of the exposition of espionage technicalities. Important for Pinter's political work of the 1980s are his slight additions of two London club scenes. In the first, two Whitehall bureaucrats exchange information over lunch, in which roast pheasant has the same significance as an agent shot through the spine by a 9.3-caliber bullet. In a second encounter one of the upper-class mandarins in full evening regalia for the Lord Mayor's Midsummer Banquet queries news from Berlin over a vodka. Immediately following this the camera shows the beaten and bedraggled body of Quiller on the edge of a river. Here, in both instances, the concrete facts of violent death and pain obtrude upon the totally removed background of so-called normality. The two extremes are necessarily linked in a chain of cause and effect, but the reality of a smashed spine and violent death is turned into a datum of ballistics. In the 1980s Pinter became publicly committed to insuring that the reality of human suffering should never become an issue for logistics. Looking ahead to 1983, this is exactly what Pinter dramatized in his sketch "Precisely," in which two bureaucrats debate the figure of "twenty million" and those who have dared suggest "thirty" or even "forty million." With the format and occasion of performance being an antinuclear show, "The Big One" at the Victoria Apollo, London, the delayed word *dead* here, though anticipated, still carries ironic shock when it comes.

In transforming Hall's thriller, Pinter accommodated the spy genre to one of his own preoccupations, which in large part grew from the cold war background to *The Birthday Party,* the close proximity of the ordinary and everyday with violence and atrocity. This is emphasized in the film by the constant recourse to the backdrop of Quiller's activities, of Berlin shops, cafés, and bars, traffic, and hotels. The key line of dialogue is that of Pol, Quiller's control, outlining the low profile of the neo-Nazis: "They're difficult to recognize—they look like everybody else" (143).

Central to Pinter's original conception, not found in Hall, is an aspect of human experience touched on throughout his work but here given a specific stress and meaning: games. Pol briefs Quiller, concerning the imperative of discovering the neo-Nazi base, in the stadium built by Hitler for the 1936 Olympics. Working from scraps of information, Quiller then follows up a clue by visiting a bowling alley. Again, he tracks Nazi associates to a palatial swimming pool, where he pretends he is a visiting swimming instructor. When he succeeds in gaining access to the Nazi base, their leader, Oktober, is practicing with a golf ball apparatus. George Segal, an actor with considerable expertise in serio-comic parts, was cast as Quiller. With his constantly wry smile, he was an ideal choice.

Amusingly irritated by control insisting that he have a cover, Quiller quickly loses him—and then joins the resigned agent, Hengel, in a bar. "You were playing a game with me" (146), Hengel says. Quiller knows that he is a pawn in a game that is deadly only for him. Pol playfully demonstrates this with two currant cakes as the opposing forces—and Quiller as the currant in the middle, which Pol eats. Earlier Quiller had pretended to be a sportswriter when visiting a school at which a master had been arrested as a former Nazi war criminal. With casual cleverness Quiller elicits the fact that Inge, a teacher, although claiming to know nothing about boxing, knows all about the Schmeling–Joe Louis fights of the Hitler era.

Quiller survives an assassination attempt and completes his mission with the Nazis rounded up, except for Inge, with whom he has reciprocally conducted an affair, and who, with other school personnel, is clearly implicated. In a film that is subtler than is usually allowed for, Quiller returns to the school for the second and final time, making his way through the groups of children on the playground, playing games. Thus, the director Michael Anderson, following the prelude of the agent's violent death, provides two frame images: the Nazi Olympic stadium and the postwar school playground. The latter suggests that the first atrocity begins in the mind, implying a chain of cause and effect from the playground to the gas chamber. As Quiller remarks, testing Inge: "They want to infiltrate themselves into the mind of the country, over a period of years. But they're not in any kind of hurry, this time" (159).

Accident (1967)

An accident may be considered as an unforeseen effect, a seemingly chance happening, outside a predictable chain of cause and effect. In terms of human behavior a degree of predictability is possible in some social circumstances, such as the cricket match in *Accident,* for example. But with the complexities of human psychology, though something might observably take place, the cause may be remote and convoluted. As Pinter put it, in discussing *Accident,* his second film with Joseph Losey: "Who are we to say that this happens because that happened, that one thing is the consequence of another? How do we know? . . . any connections we think we see, or choose to make, are pure guesswork."[3]

In some respects, though this is applicable to much of Pinter's writing, it seems initially questionable in relation to *Accident,* in which the beautiful Anna, an aristocratic Austrian student who arrives at an Oxford college, immediately acts as an erotic catalyst for three men—Stephen, her philosophy tutor, William, a fellow aristocrat and student, and Charley, a populist television academic.

A fatal accident opens and closes the film. Crashing outside Stephen's country house, William is killed because of Anna's driving, a fact that Stephen hides from the police in order to coerce her into sex immediately that night. Though unofficially engaged to William, Anna had entered into an affair with Charley. Thus, the three men are rivals—intellectually, socially, sexually, and professionally. There are variables in a causal pattern. William has youth and blueblood fortune; Charley has the macho charisma of a successful TV don; Stephen has intellect and seeming probity, until he attempts to rival Charley in populism.

Understanding of causality may be traced back to Aristotle, who figures in a Senior Common Room joke, inserted by Pinter: "A statistical analysis of sexual intercourse among students at Colenso University, Milwaukee, showed that 70 per cent did it in the morning, 29.9 per cent between two and four in the afternoon and 0.1 per cent during a lecture on Aristotle," Charley reads out. Unfazed, the Provost replies, "I'm surprised to hear Aristotle is on the syllabus in the state of Wisconsin" (233). The anecdote and joke bring together mind and body, speech and action, cause and effect. Ironically, it is Stephen, also listening, who slept with the Provost's daughter before his marriage and briefly resumes that activity on his London visit to rival Charley on TV (and in bed, it would seem).

The advent of Anna makes apparent the thinness of all the seemingly solid middle-class and aristocratic values around them—learning and civility, family and faithfulness—all centered in hospitality. Anna's arrival is an accident, not a necessary occurrence; to what takes place thereafter she can only be a contributory factor, releasing what is latent, not creating it.

Stephen invites Anna and William to Sunday lunch, ostensibly to meet his wife and children, but the gathering is gate-crashed by the familiarly boorish Charley, and eventually turns from civility and friendship to a day-long drunken bout, as the men grow to recognize their mutual desire and rivalry. William collapses in an alcoholic stupor at supper, which is presided over by Stephen's wife, as cautious pregnant matriarch, and later, it is revealed, Charley betrays friendship and hospitality by opportunistically sleeping with Anna. Alcohol debases the mind, the body, and hospitality, and this is structurally reciprocated in Stephen's visit as houseguest to William's upper-crust baroque mansion in the debasement of aristocratic ritual.

Ideally chosen as the location, Syon House provided an elegant interior of neoclassical proportion, measure, and balance—so rudely shattered by the mock-Etonian game that takes place in the palatial hall. This domesticized animality masquerading as indoor rugby, if anything, was slightly underdone by Losey. Pinter's camera directions reveal his own revulsion: "*A scrum. . . . A communal buggery. . . . He cracks his elbows sharply into the faces of two others . . . butts the fourth* MAN *with his head . . . arms flailing, bodies twisting . . . elbows . . . kicking . . . cuffing . . . scrum. . . . It strives forward ponderously, brokenly: a bowel with a gut gone*" (270–71). As this takes place, Charley is copulating with Anna, in Stephen's otherwise empty house, with his connivance. The scene cuts to a college cricket match, in which William and Charley are playing, and Anna approaches Stephen and says, "Thank you for your hospitality," in response to his loaded question, "Have a nice week-end?" (273).

The style of the film was in direct contrast to the baroque, with Losey's direction stressing the linear and horizontal throughout—fields, the front elevation of Stephen's Georgian country house, dining tables, and cricket field. This visual style complemented Pinter's dialogue, which was almost wholly and deliberately concerned with reflecting social surface and exchange. Arriving at Oxford to shoot the film, Losey found in medieval architecture the image that would deftly comment on words and actions, the gargoyles outside Stephen's study. Close-ups showed beasts and humans in grotesque physical contortions, in contrast to Stephen's new baby at the end of the film, which arrives, surviving a tricky birth, as Anna departs after a tragic death, both subject to cause, effect, and accident.

Notes

1. David Caute "Golden Triangle," *The Independent on Sunday, The Sunday Review,* 7 November 1993, 24. From Caute's forthcoming study *Joseph Losey: A Revenge on Life* (London: Faber, 1994).

2. *Ibid.*

3. John Russell Taylor, "Accident," *Sight and Sound* 35, no. 4 (1966): 184.

CHAPTER FIVE

The Homecoming (1965)

One day Pinter was told the story of someone from his kind of background who left home for the United States, did well, married and had children, and suddenly returned with his wife without telling anyone. The anecdote sunk into the unconscious, and then, in due course, a play was engendered. Many would regard *The Homecoming* as Pinter's greatest achievement. Indeed, some would regard it as among the greatest plays of the twentieth century. Without doubt it may be grouped with Pinter's most famous plays, yet in its day *The Homecoming* was regarded by some critics as cynical, obscene, and degrading.

Teddy, a lecturer in philosophy, returns with Ruth to the all-male household of his brothers Lenny, a pimp, and Joey, a demolition worker; Uncle Sam, a chauffeur; and Max, his father, a retired butcher. The unexpected return provokes a mixed reaction, but it is far from the sentimental coziness of welcome implied by the title. In very broad terms it can be said that Pinter's play, along with various other art forms of the twentieth century, is written out of a strong sense of distaste for the culture of sentimentality which colored much nineteenth-century art and subsequently became a potent factor of popular twentieth-century culture, particularly in the cinema and the musical theater—above all in periods conducive to escapist entertainment, such as the postwar years of 1920–30 and 1945–60. Sentimentality is, indeed, an element of *The Homecoming,* but it is subjected to the most extreme of reversals, such as the close, when Ruth is invited by the family to remain as a prostitute domestically and publicly.

The Homecoming has a radical greatness in the way it confronts assumptions about the idea of the nuclear family, and thus of twentieth-century Western society, and reexamines what is found. The ideal facade consists of love, care, and kindness, responsibility, dignity, and commitment, but the reality may be considerably less than this. The small detail of Joey, the younger brother, as a laborer in the demolition business is very important for Pinter's conception of the play as a whole. The experience of *The Homecoming* is like knocking down an old building, clearing the rubble, and examining just what the foundations are made of. Certainly scarifying in places, the play is not finally cynical. Although humanity can undergo deprivation and distortion, in the midst of seeming perversity, at the close an ineradicable human need survives. There is ugliness and dismay but not just that: there is the need for love, though dumb and crippled, but hardly of the Dickensian kind.

The following analysis of *The Homecoming* will develop from three different standpoints. First, some ground needs to be cleared concerning the topic discussed in chapter 1, the question of "realistic," "realism," and "reality." Once it is grasped that a work of art can represent different kinds of reality at the same time, then it is possible to move on to the issue of structure, style, and formalization. A first impression of the play may seem to be overwhelmingly naturalistic, but a further more penetrating overview will show how the play is entirely structured, from one line to the work as a whole, by a principle of binary opposition in which drama derives from the interaction of a series of polar opposites. This concept from the theory of structuralism will be seen to be immensely fruitful not only in the play but also as a constituent element of Pinter's creative imagination. It is worth noting Pinter's remark of 1966: "The only play which gets remotely near to a structural entity which satisfies me is *The Homecoming*."[1] Third, this structuralist position will be re-examined in the light of Freud's theories on male sexuality, particularly his focus of the male impulse to degrade the female.

One of the vexed problems of literature, theory, and criticism is that it isn't really possible to get along without the word *reality,* yet, ironically, as soon as it is introduced, it seems to raise more questions than it answers. Whenever the word is used as a singular noun, it implies a unilateral view of the subject. From certain positions of an extreme kind—for example, those of a priest or physicist—this might well be insisted on: Reality as God, or Energy. But it is necessary to consider the idea of reality more pluralistically, as consisting of several realities. Few people would take exception to discussion of such concepts as political or economic reality. Considering realities and the individual, it would not be difficult to find some agreement. To deny a reality to environment, the reality of material surroundings, hardly seems sane. As a corollary of this, there is social being, the objective actuality of the self and interrelationships at work, at home, and in the community. To complement these external realities there is the subjective inner reality of selfhood—of such things as beliefs, hopes, dreams, and feelings.

Here lies the problem. To juggle with Orwellian phraseology: all things are real, but some things are more real than others. In different situations the claim of one kind of reality might seem greater than another. There is not necessarily a fixed hierarchy of realities, though many might insist that the psychological reality of the individual is paramount. Conversely, part of the heritage of romanticism is that the experience of the artist, transmuted into art, offers the greatest reality since, by virtue of genius, reality is thereby made manifest, often by symbolism, the vehicle of a transcendental reality. Where the greater reality of one thing is granted, then, the lesser reality of another is implied, hence the hierarchy previously mentioned. And then this whole stable positivist approach can be shaken by the admission that what seems real can become unreal, particularly within the ineluctable dimension of time. This is a major aspect of Pinter's memory plays.

The selection and representation of any particular kind, or kinds, of reality in drama will depend on the relationship of convention and style to the cultural moment, within a spectrum of relative influences and values, not least of which is censorship. In short, what might seem very realistic in one decade can, in retrospect, seem relatively formalized, or even unreal, in another. Thus, the realism of the 1950s kitchen-sink dramatists seems almost stagy by later standards. Applying these considerations to *The Homecoming,* certain discriminations can be made without which, as in some early audiences, the ending might seem objectionably bizarre, unreal, and thus unacceptable.

At the outset the play appears to be grounded in the domestic realism of an urban sitting room, which is seemingly corroborated by the colloquial London speech:

> MAX: . . . Do you hear what I'm saying? I'm talking to you!
> Where's the scissors?
> LENNY: (*looking up, quietly*) Why don't you shut up, you daft
> prat?

(15)

As the action proceeds with the entries of the other members of the family, Joey and Sam, an all-male household is presented, in which aggravation, sarcasm, and provocation have become entirely habitual. After a blackout, without any expository anticipation, Teddy and Ruth appear. Within a page or so of dialogue Teddy directs Ruth's and the audience's attention to something of an oddity of the room's structure—the rear wall is missing: "Actually there was a wall, across there . . . with a door. We knocked it down . . . years ago . . . to make an open living area. The structure wasn't affected, you see. My mother was dead" (29). This correlation of the physical and emotional is emphatically and overtly symbolic—so much so that in the original production the set designer, John Bury, with Pinter's approval, left the load-supporting beam exposed.[2] This huge gap in all their lives was further symbolized in the original production by an almost colorless set, which was recreated by the same director, Peter Hall, for the 1991 London production in honor of Pinter's sixtieth birthday. What is dimly latent in this sterile set is hinted at in Teddy's nervous speech, and the audience response is accordingly deepened by apprehension and confirmed by the defamatory attacks, directly and indirectly, on Ruth, the lone woman surrounded by womenless men. At this point, however, the movement combining the realistic with the symbolic is hardly unusual but, rather, is quite typical of much twentieth-century drama. What audiences found too outrageous to accept was the final action of the second half.

Act 2 starts solidly with after-dinner coffee being distributed and cozy sentimental recall—but not for long. Shortly, the antagonism and sarcasm return in language, but, as Teddy and Ruth are preparing for departure, the action also becomes bizarre. As Teddy "*stands, with* RUTH*'s coat*" (66), looking on, Lenny dances with Ruth and kisses her. Joey thus encouraged takes Ruth to the sofa, "*embraces and kisses her.*" Lenny then caresses her at the same time. As the erotic action continues, the stage direction is crucial: "JOEY *lies heavily on* RUTH. *They are almost still.* LENNY *caresses her hair*" (67). Thus, the arrested movement of Joey and Ruth presents a formalized, nonnaturalistic pose. Immediately, the following sequence of stage directions occurs:

> JOEY *and* RUTH *roll off the sofa on to the floor.*
> JOEY *clasps her.* LENNY *moves to stand above them. He looks down on them. He touches* RUTH *gently with his foot.* RUTH *suddenly pushes* JOEY *away. She stands up.*
> JOEY *gets to his feet, stares at her.* (68)

The erotic is almost compromised by farce here because, while this is happening, Max is talking to Teddy paternally as if nothing untoward were happening and it was the most normal situation in the world. This aspect of the bizarre is then dramatically furthered by Ruth virtually taking charge and beginning to order the men around. While the men talk, Ruth disappears upstairs for two hours with Joey, yet Teddy is seemingly undisturbed. Upon returning, she is propositioned by the family to stay on as a prostitute and communal concubine. The play closes with an all-important tableau, like that of Joey over Ruth, which must be returned to with discussion of Freud.

Many have rejected all this as unreal. Others have lamely accommodated it with the label "surreal." If an earlier part of the discussion is returned to, it is possible to arrive at greater insight. *The Homecoming* at the outset largely depicts an external social reality of domestic relationships. Subjective reality, at this stage, is only hinted at—what did the death of Jessie, wife and mother, mean for them all? The entry of Ruth, another wife and mother, exacerbates this question and brings into conflict two planes of reality, the social and the psychological. Pinter's technique is to intercut and juxtapose each until one becomes a critique of the other. Psychological reality subverts the social reality in which Teddy in fact hides, refusing in his cold intellectuality to be drawn further. As in twentieth-century graphic art, one plane is superimposed on another. By the final tableau the innermost conflicting subjectivity of debasement and love is externalized, exposed, and objectified, creating one of the most powerful conclusions of modern drama. If the play is now reexamined in terms of style and structure, it will be shown how these planes of reality are highly formalized throughout by a thoroughgoing structuralist mode in the concept of binary opposition.

Structuralism, as a method, derives from the development of modern linguistics in Ferdinand de Saussure and gradually spread to other disciplines such as sociology and literary theory, but perhaps most impressively in the anthropology of Claude Lévi-Strauss.[3] Lévi-Strauss took Saussure's fundamental binary concept of the signifier and the signified and applied it to primitive society and myth, studying such oppositions as the raw and the cooked, noise and silence, rotten and burned. To apply a reversed analogy, a native visiting a modern city would have little grasp of its organization without an understanding of the various underground networks providing power and transport, all regulated according to the permissible and its opposite. Structuralism locates the meaning of any given phenomenon in relation to a larger underlying structure of meaning, and this is often found to be organized on a binary principle of polar opposition which is thought to reflect that of the nature of mind itself. It is not difficult to glance at human culture to find such oppositions, since they appear to constitute thought and being itself—namely, such pairings as mind and body, reason and passion, good and evil. Structuralism can enrich, or it can be dryly reductive, depending on its application. Here, obviously, as a second stage of investigation looking more closely at the detail of the text, it is embarked on in the belief that it does indeed get closer to the complexities of *The Homecoming.*

As a prefatory observation, it could be claimed that Pinter's creative imagination is fundamentally binary, since at the core of nearly all his work are theatricality and realism, laughter and seriousness. In *The Homecoming* an oscillating mesh of interacting oppositions are found at any given moment. To a great extent conflict defines much drama, nowhere more so than here, where multiple conflicts proliferate with the ceaseless interaction of such oppositions as civility and animality, domesticity and violence, sentimentality and sexuality. In turn these are linked to male and female, self and family, praise and denigration.

For example, consider the opening of the play. Max enters looking for scissors; Lenny is reading a newspaper. Ordinary domesticity is challenged by Lennie's rudeness, but he remains immersed in his newspaper, generally ignoring his father, which of course acts as a provocation and draws the following from Max: "You think I wasn't a tearaway? I could have taken care of you, twice over. I'm still strong. You ask your Uncle Sam what I was. But at the same time I always had a kind heart. Always" (16). Within the domestic setting token violence is threatened and augmented in the first two lines given here. Yet the preceding confession of age, "I'm getting old, my word of honour," and the fact that Max carries a walking stick while searching for scissors to cut out an advertisement for "flannel vests," tends to undermine, comically, the claim "I'm still strong." Maleness is asserted in the word *tearaway* to counter Lennie's denigratory remark, "you daft prat" (15). The next line concerning "Uncle Sam" invokes family relationship for the first time in a way that is important for the play as a whole. Here the opposition between domesticity and violence shifts to that of the family as violence and the family as love. Uncle Sam's status within the family is ironically adduced to authenticate paternal threat in the present by testifying to real violence in the past, and appealed to, in implicit honorific terms, as a reminder to the son/nephew of his place within a hierarchy—unlike Teddy, whom we see has opted out. Max's implicit appeal to family, which invalidates the threatening polarity of self and family, is strengthened insidiously as he shifts to sentimentality: "But at the same time I always had a kind heart. Always."

Analysis of a large-scale example in the sequences that close act 1 and open act 2 (47–56) will bring out this mode most tellingly. Max's serious sentimental recall in praise of his dying father, "When Dad died he said to me, Max, look after your brothers," is punctured by the humor of Sam's question, "How could he speak if he was dead?" and is turned to denigration against his brother, "You wet wick" (47), followed by an astounding image compounding reverence, animality, and violence: "I learned to carve a carcase at his knee. I commemorated his name in blood." The speech culminates in an image of role reversal which is part of the male-female opposition throughout the play: "I gave birth to three grown men! All on my own bat. What have you done?" Conversely, sexual reversal (Sam is shortly decried as a homosexual) and denigration is compacted into "You tit!" Then Max reverts to the familial line "After all, we are brothers" (48). With the descent of Teddy and Ruth from the bedroom the son's familial address, "Dad," is swept aside by overwhelming denigration, the male verbally attacking the female ("dirty tarts . . . smelly scrubber . . . stinking pox-ridden slut" [49]). As with Sam, Teddy is rounded on in sexually inverted terms as "the bitch." And then the vituperative includes the familial, and both are temporarily collapsed in humor: "I've never had a whore under this roof before. Ever since your mother died." Yet prostitution and motherhood are to be most seriously superimposed in the final tableau of the play. Actual violence then takes place as Max reacts to Joey's "He's an old man" (50) by punching him in the stomach and then hitting Sam on the head with his stick. The act closes on a reversal of the heavily sentimental and familial. Ruth's vilified sexuality is transformed into sentimental motherhood, "You a mother?" (51), and Max and Teddy prepare for a "cuddle" as the curtain is brought down on Max's line "He still loves his father" (52).

Act 2 opens with the long-drawn-out stage business of the civility of after-dinner coffee and the mutual praise of Max and Ruth. Max then launches into an anecdotal panegyric on family life, the sentimentality of which indirectly calls into question the exact nature of whatever was the past reality:

> . . . and I said to her, Jessie, I think our ship is going to come home, I'm going to treat you to a couple of items, I'm going to buy you a dress in pale corded blue silk, heavily encrusted in pearls, and for casual wear, a pair of pantaloons in lilac flowered taffeta. Then I gave her a drop of cherry brandy. I remember the boys came down, in their pyjamas, all their hair shining, their faces pink . . . and they knelt down at our feet, Jessie's and mine. (54)

Then suddenly a question from Ruth triggers a reversal. The "first-class cigar" (21) of act 1 becomes "a lousy cigar," and the idealized family becomes "a crippled family, three bastard sons, a slutbitch of a wife" (55). Sexually suggestive denigration hurled at Sam is made explicit in the charge "You'd bend over for half a dollar on Blackfriars Bridge," the sexually passive female role quite at odds with Sam's subsequent claim to have fought in the war, which is quashed by the violence of Max's question "Who did you kill?" Familial sentimentality immediately succeeds this, with "Well, how you been keeping, son?" (56). In going to

America, Teddy asserted himself against the family that, in *The Homecoming,* always makes a claim greater than the individual ego. Familial names recur more than one hundred and thirty times in the play, yet, in terms of the binary opposition of praise and denigration, to revere or to revile, affirmation of family is equally undermined by subjecting it to the multiple oppositions found within domesticity, civility, and sentimentality assaulted by sexuality, violence, and animality. In the repeated use of familial terms—primarily *family, dad, father, mother, mum, son, brother, wife, uncle*—every family relationship is systematically mocked and scorned. Although these names are diffused throughout the play, Pinter often dramatizes this mockery by grouping terms for a binary effect, which generates an extremely powerful irony. One example, when Teddy declines to offer money to support Ruth as a prostitute in the London ménage-menagerie, Max explodes: "What? You won't even help to support your own wife? I though he was a son of mine. You lousy stinkpig. Your mother would drop dead if she heard you taking that attitude" (79).[4]

As the play unfolds, it becomes apparent that within the praise and denigration polarity is the figure of the woman as mother and whore, which calls for the third stage of interpretation by moving into the territory of Freud. Freudian psychoanalysis has probably been the most prevalent form of applied literary criticism in this century, particularly in the United States, where, for a time, it was almost institutional. Unsurprisingly, Freud is often introduced into discussion of *The Homecoming* and is found in Martin Esslin's early study, in which he suggests: "From the sons' point of view therefore, *The Homecoming* is a dream image of the fulfilment of all Oedipal wishes, the sexual conquest of the mother, the utter humiliation of the father. From the father's point of view the play is the terrifying nightmare of the sons' revenge."[5] A different Freudian reading will be offered here, developing from the structuralist examination and drawing on a particular study of Freud's, the second of his *Contributions to the Psychology of Love*—namely, "On the Universal Tendency to Debasement in the Sphere of Love" (1912).[6] Before doing so, further evidence from the play should be considered with that previously adduced.

Max is foremost in his vilification of Jessie and Ruth, her reincarnation, as "whores," whereas Lenny provides an anecdotal framework by which all women may be seen in this light. In his story of the prostitute "down by the docks" Lenny claims that "the only trouble was she was falling apart with the pox," and thus the story of his vicious attack, after which Ruth calmly inquires: "How did you know she was diseased?" Lennie's answer suggests his deterministic view of women generally: "I decided she was" (38–39). Later Lenny enlists Joey in the story of their North Paddington jaunt, in which they virtually abducted two girls from their boyfriends and forced them to have sex on a bombed site, "in the rubble." "Yes, plenty of rubble" (75), as Lenny gleefully adds. Max's language, Lennie's allusions to the prostitute and her chauffeur, and Sam's anecdotes of his chauffeuring Jessie all build up the insinuation that she might have been considerably less than the ideal mother-wife, and Sam's final revelation, if it is true, seems to confirm this: "MacGregor had Jessie in the back of my cab as I drove them along" (86).

Until the later movement toward the final tableau what is found is the collective impulse to degrade womanhood, to debase the female by insisting on whoredom as a lowest common denominator. Freud's study of debasement derived from the empirical work on his case histories during consultation in Vienna. He observed the frequency with which otherwise respectable and seemingly happily married men with attractive wives nevertheless commonly resorted to prostitutes. In Freud's understanding, these men are driven to debasement because only in this way can they fully realize sexual intercourse. That is, only by separating sensuality from emotion, eroticism from tenderness, are they able to fulfill physical sex. These men cannot combine the physical drives and affective needs with the same person, thereby transforming sex into love. Freud's explanation for this is the incest taboo. In his study of male development he observed that the early figures associated with the male child's emotional stability were all versions of the mother figure—sister, nurse, and so on. With the onset of adolescence and sexual maturity, sensuality clashed with the earlier established channels of affection and was blocked by psychical impotence. Only by debasement could it be freed. Thus, these men were perpetually denied the possibility of a fully realized love, and Freud encapsulated this in a tragic paradox: "Where they love they do not desire and where they desire they cannot love."[7]

The theory of the incest taboo does not have to be accepted, though much anthropological study might support it. What is of importance here is the manifest impulse to degrade the female found in *The Homecoming* in relation to the desperate need for love which Freud identifies and its thwarted end. But debasement, with Ruth as some kind of imperious whore reigning supreme, is not the end of the play. An understanding of the final tableau, in relation to the rest of the play, is of the utmost importance, and it is Joey who is the key figure.

Joey, the demolition worker and boxer manqué, is relatively
inarticulate in comparison with the others. As a consequence, in
studying the text, his significance can be easily overlooked without the focus being on action in performance. Witnessing Lenny
dancing and kissing Ruth, Joey exclaims, "Christ, she's wide
open," and then, after a pause, "She's a tart" (66), and he acts
accordingly by taking her over, embracing her, and kissing her
sordidly in front of Teddy, but only up to a point, since Pinter
formalizes movement: "JOEY *lies heavily on* RUTH. *They are almost still*" (67). This is protracted onstage until they "*roll off the
sofa on to the floor*" (68). As with Teddy's earlier remarks on the
missing wall, Pinter is signaling the juxtaposition of planes of
reality. Thereafter, Joey says next to nothing, but Pinter indicates the development of what is a kind of awakening: "JOEY
moves towards her"; "JOEY *moves closer to* RUTH" (68, 69).

When Joey comes down, leaving Ruth upstairs, he is som-
nolent and defensive about his lack of sexual conquest. This leads
Lenny to recount the story of the North Paddington foray, with
all its detailed sordidness. Joey's comment at the end of it, provided by Lennie's incredulous "Don't tell me you're satisfied
without going the whole hog?" (76), is remarkable, not least
because, following a pause, it is the longest speech by him in the
play: "I've been the whole hog plenty of times. Sometimes . . .
you can be happy . . . and not go the whole hog. Now and again
. . . you can be happy . . . without going any hog" (76). Joey's
gauche presence, his clumsy limbering-up exercises, and Max's
facetious remarks can often make him a comic butt. In the 1978
revival at the Garrick, at the opening of act 2, assisting with the
coffee, he was portrayed as a late 1950s "Teddy boy" complete

with heavily crepe-soled suede shoes, known as "brothel-creepers" in the day, to the great amusement of the audience. Yet Joey has undergone an inchoate awakening.

Joey stumbles repetitiously around the only word he can find: *happy.* He rejects the thought of Ruth with Teddy. He offers to give money and to buy clothes, slow-wittedly unaware of quite what is going on, which, when he discovers the nature of the proposal, is rejected: "I didn't think I was going to have to share her!" (81). Finally, Joey *"walks slowly across the room. He kneels at her chair. She touches his head, lightly. He puts his head in her lap"* (88). Max crawls toward her, both begging and demanding "Kiss me" (90), the last words of the play, while *"She continues to touch* JOEY's *head, lightly while* LENNY *stands, watching"* and intransigent. In this tableau atavistic abasement cannot expunge the need for love. In the midst of debasement Ruth acts out the facts and fantasies of male obsessions, fears, and privation; though evidently a whore for Lenny, for Max she is a lover and for Joey a mother. Ruth is ultimately redemptive. Like the supporting beam, she saves them from the "rubble."

Notes

1. "Harold Pinter: An Interview" (with Lawrence Bensky), in *Pinter: A Collection of Critical Essays,* edited by Arthur Ganz (Englewood Cliffs, N.J.: Prentice-Hall, 1972), 26.

2. John Lahr, ed., *A Casebook on Harold Pinter's "The Homecoming"* (New York: Grove Press, 1971), 28.

3. See Dan Sperber, "Claude Lévi-Strauss," in John Sturrock, ed., *Structuralism and Since* (Oxford: Oxford University Press, 1979), 19–51.

4. In fact the line "I thought he was a son of mine" was cut by Pinter from the current Faber edition and from the older Eyre Methuen's *Plays Three*. This text is found in the Methuen single volume edition of 1972, page 71.

5. Martin Esslin, *Pinter: A Study of His Plays* (London and New York: Eyre Methuen, 1977), 155.

6. *On Sexuality,* The Pelican Freud Library, vol. 7 (Harmondsworth, 1912), 243–60.

7. *Ibid.,* 251.

CHAPTER SIX

Plays, 1967–81:
Landscape, Silence, Old Times, No Man's Land, Monologue, Betrayal, Other Places

The experience of writing *The Homecoming,* with its de-mands on all of Pinter's resources of imagination and language, drained the writer of creative energy for a few years until *Land-scape* (1968), which proved to inaugurate a major development in his work. *Landscape, Silence* (1969), *Old Times* (1971), and *No Man's Land* (1975) are usually categorized as Pinter's "memory plays." The revue sketch "Night" (1969) may be added to this group, and the screenplays considered in another chap-ter—*Langrishe, Go Down* (written 1971, produced 1978), *The Go-Between* (1971), and *The Proust Screenplay* (1972)—all bear the marks of Pinter's preoccupation with memory.

Landscape (1968)

Landscape was originally presented on the radio in 1968, since the Lord Chamberlain refused to license the play for the stage because of one obscenity. Such was Pinter's integrity and insistence on the precise necessity of the individual word that he refused to alter it. Coincidently, the role of public censor was withdrawn in the same year, and *Landscape* and *Silence* appeared onstage as a double bill in 1969. The immediate critical response was to compare these works with Beckett, and, although *Old Times* modified this view, there was some justification at that particular moment. In short, as in Beckett's plays after the 1950s, Pinter's dramatic minimalism here strives for the maximum effect from the barest resource of theater.

In conception, design, and movement, *Landscape* dramatizes separation. The set separates Beth and Duff as they sit throughout at each end of "*a long kitchen table*" (166). The curtain rises on a kitchen of a country house, but the seeming initial realism characteristic of all Pinter's plays until now is immediately compromised by the speech, as indicated in a prefatory note: "DUFF *refers normally to* BETH, *but does not appear to hear her voice.* BETH *never looks at* DUFF, *and does not appear to hear his voice*" (166). Beth's speech evokes the surfacing fragments of an interior monologue concerning the past, a beach, and love; Duff refers to the mundane events of yesterday. Beth reveals a subjective world of feelings, Duff an objective catalog of things.

As in *The Homecoming,* two planes of reality are paralleled, the psychological and the social, which are emphasized by the parallel modes of address, or nonaddress, and the shape of the table. Old-style country house tables are extremely long, and the rectangular shape and placing of the chairs provides a source of drama in the visual image—will the parallel lines of dialogue, like the positioning of Beth and Duff, never meet? At first the answer seems to be certainly not, as the style and content of each is so opposed. Beth's soliloquy is juxtaposed and intercut between Duff's half of an unanswered conversation.

Beth with an artist's aesthetic imagination evokes the fineness and delicacy of "touch" and the beach. Duff's crudeness recalls "dogshit, duckshit . . . all kinds of shit" (170), in the park. Yet even here there is a tactile quality in both, a quality that is central in Beth's aestheticization of the sensual and a gesture that precedes Duff's admission of betrayal: "I touched you" (177). Demanding great concentration in his audience, Pinter derives drama from ironic resonance, as the following has just been heard from Beth:

> He followed me and watched, standing at a distance from me. When the arrangement was done I stayed still, I heard him moving. He didn't touch me. I listened. I looked at the flowers, blue and white, in the bowl.
> *Pause.*
> Then he touched me.
> *Pause.*
> He touched the back of my neck. His fingers, lightly, touching, lightly touching, the back, of my neck. (171)

Beth is associated with the sky and the sea in the blue and white of flowers and dress, whereas Duff always returns to the excremental ("The dregs'll give you the shits" [184]). Yet Pinter orchestrates parallelism in a suggestive way in allusions that seem increasingly to be near collision as the following examples show: "DUFF: There wasn't a soul in the park"; "BETH: There wasn't a soul on the beach" (171); "BETH: Snoozing how lovely I said to him"; "Duff: I'm sleeping all right these days" (172); "Beth: I knew there must be a hotel near"; "Duff: The pubs were open" (173). An all-important connection is made, but Pinter chooses to keep it indirect to reflect separation, thus the following quotations are separated by six pages of text: "Beth: My gravity, he said. I was so grave, attending to the flowers" (170–71); "Duff: You were . . . grave" (176).

This allusive identification of Duff as Beth's earlier lover remains such as the exclusive parallelism is reaffirmed in the contrast between Duff's practical lesson on a pub cellar man's job, "The bung is on the vertical, in the bunghole" (183), and Beth's rehearsal of the artistic "principles of shadow and light" (185–86). Separation becomes absolute as Duff's sexually charged language explodes with the enraged impotence of rejection: "Mind you don't get the scissors up your arse" (187). With gently lyrical recollection of fulfilled love, Beth concludes, "Oh my true love I said" (188). Duff was her tender love, yet he has declined so grossly, while Beth's lover in memory is like her drawing, a selective idealized figure in a landscape of the mind, providing psychological compensation for her unhappiness. The drama of verification can be contrasted with that of *The Collection* and compared to that of *Silence*.

Silence (1969)

Pinter recorded that *Silence* had taken longer to write than any earlier piece, although it is a short work. The play is possibly Pinter's most abstract and difficult at a first approach, but

aspects of production immediately begin to resolve seeming problems. One of the most discussed characteristics of Pinter's work
is his dramatic exploitation of pause and silence. The dramatist
wrote of speech as "a constant stratagem to cover nakedness."[1]
Silence exposes self and others. People often only half-listen to
those around them, and this habit can be carried into the theater—but an audience listens closely to silence, which creates
multiple responses: What is happening? What happened? What
will they say? What will they do? In these moments the characters are suspended in the interstices of existence, where being
takes precedence over doing. Staging this is to push drama to its
limits, and that is what *Silence* achieves.

There is no set for the play. There are simply three chairs
for the three characters, each in a clearly defined area of the
stage. The separation found in *Landscape* is taken a step further.
The dramatis personae gives "ELLEN: *a girl in her twenties,*
RUMSEY: *a man of forty, and* BATES: *a man in his middle thirties*"
(190). An actual production, like that of the Open University,
makes plain what might evade a reader of the text: each character speaks with two voices, one as indicated and another as much
as thirty years older. Onstage, as against radio, this technique
could run the risk of an inadvertent ventriloquism, depending on
the actor's subtlety. The structure of *Silence* begins with the young
and old voices of Ellen and Bates alternating around silences.
On the three occasions only when one character turns to another,
the younger voice is heard. Speech patterns are laid down in
both younger and older voices, with Ellen's unfulfilled association with the paternal Rumsey, Rumsey's stoically fortified loneliness, and Bates's antiromantic crudities. As the play unfolds,

patterns of repetition recur in increasing fragments of the young and old voices, thus making the silences more and more frequent, with fragments in turn fragmenting further around silence. Separation becomes a more complex dislocation that is temporal, spatial, and psychological. The movement from *The Homecoming* to *Landscape* and *Silence* is toward concentration on another plane of reality, that of memory, on which being, self, and identity become truncated fragments. For example, compare the following speeches of Ellen:

> Around me sits the night. Such a silence. I can hear myself. Cup my ear. My heart beats in my ear. Such a silence. Is it me? Am I silent or speaking? How can I know. Can I know such things? No-one has ever told me, I need to be told things. I seem to be old. Am I old now? No-one will tell me. I must find a person to tell me these things. (201)

> *Silence.*
> Around me sits the night. Such a silence. (207)

Evasion of communication is carried to a final logical conclusion with the breakdown of *self*-communication. The characters in their isolation do not even have the relative solidity of those early rooms. *Silence* stands in direct antithesis to the nineteenth-century novel's celebration of the concrete unitary ego. Being as merely speech is eclipsed by an enveloping *Silence*. On the one hand, such expression is as close as Pinter gets to spiritual bereftness; on the other, in this as in many of his works, his creative intuitions reflect so many of the concerns of philosophers, linguists, and psychologists in the second half of the twentieth century. An inheritance of Saussure's linguistic theory has been the concept that the self does not speak language so much as language speaks the self. Such traditional ideas as "soul" and "spirit," closely allied to the development of bourgeois individualism, are rejected by the conceptions of what is called the materialist philosophical approach. The post-Marxism of a philosopher such as Louis Althusser refines Saussure by taking such thought a stage further, in the view that culture "speaks us": individual personality becomes the site of various ideological discourses.

Reconsider someone such as Tony in *The Servant.* He is not a caricature or puppet, yet his speech, appearance, dress, manners, and gestures all give expression to the assumptions of power and ownership, the residual ideology of a ruling upper class. In some ways it could be argued that Pinter's exploration of language, being, and consciousness in *Silence* and in the epiphanic revue sketches parallels the thought of another French philosopher, Jacques Lacan. Lacan believed that the structure of the unconscious was reflected by language. With Ellen in *Silence* and the characters of the revue sketches it is as if part of Pinter's insight here was a glimpse beyond the individual "ego" into the nature of mind itself, only to find that it is a contingent series of syntactic reflexes, not so much the ghost in the machine as the machine in the ghost.

Brief discussion of "Dialogue for Three," the radio sketch taken originally from *The Hothouse,* has been delayed until this point since it clearly foreshadows *Landscape* and *Silence* as a remarkable experimental piece. On radio the original speakers in the play become disembodied voices. As such, they are used by Pinter to explore the intersecting planes of past and present at a point of anecdotal collision and fragmentation. The concrete world of character and environment—public school, the club, the army, the bedroom—is atomized, time and space are divided, and the voices are like random radio signals crossing in the atmosphere, a comic and yet haunting image of human isolation.

Old Times (1971)

Where Pinter differs very sharply from the language and thought of linguists, psychoanalysts, and philosophers is in his artistic commitment to the affective aspect of experience, the emotions, and often the fear of the destructive power of emotion. One of the most heightened emotional moments in all of Pinter's work is that experienced by Deeley, after his wife's, Kate's, symbolic rejection of him, at the end of *Old Times*.

The apparent opening realism of *Old Times,* both in set and language—a sitting room in a converted farmhouse and desultory exchanges about the impending visit of Anna, a friend of twenty years ago—is compromised by a female figure at the rear of the stage, her back to the audience, looking out of a window. In Peter Hall's original production of 1971 the figure, who neither moves nor says anything for a considerable time, was wearing a Dior dress strongly evocative of the postwar period. In contrast, the clothing of Deeley and Kate was contemporary. When the figure does turn, sweeping downstage delivering a highly mannered lyrical account of postwar friendship, it is, of course, Anna. Pinter consistently gives Anna's dialogue a literary, urbane, self-conscious formality, in contrast to Deeley's informal colloquialism, which becomes part of the ensuing language struggle for the possession of Kate. The first act ends with a seeming reversion to the past, as if Anna and Kate are sharing their flat together, as Anna asks: "Would you like me to ask someone over? . . . Charley . . . or Jake?" (41). Conversely, at the close of the play the reenactment of a past incident of rejection related by Anna in act 1 is anticipated by the bedroom furniture in the second act, reversing that of the first.

To understand Pinter's dramatic mode here it might help if his play is simplified by recreating it as a straightforward realist work. In this the old friend would arrive, and, in recalling old times, strains in Kate and Deeley's marriage would be exacerbated by his jealousy and resentment, as the friends' close intimacy becomes apparent. Peripeteia, catastrophe, and denouement would take place as Kate makes plain that friendship is a thing of the past only and that her marriage itself has reached a point of no return: curtain. But Pinter provides something infinitely more complex and suggestive. Essentially, a form is found to dramatize the psychology of memory. Anna avers: "There are some things one remembers even though they may never have happened. There are things I remember which may never have happened but as I recall them so they take place" (27–28). Memory can be fallible, and memory can be accurate, but how can the difference be known for certain, since even when there is seeming verification the corroborator may be either accurate or fallible or else merely compliant? If, in addition to this, it is acknowledged that the "reality" of the past can dominate the present, then the dramatic purpose of Pinter's mixed mode becomes apparent. The Anna of twenty years ago is made literally present as she is recalled in memory. When Anna seems to be winning the struggle for Kate, the past prevails over the present and is reenacted onstage. The plane of memory finds a dramatic fourth dimension beyond that of three-dimensional realism.

Examination of a sequence (22–28) will bring out some of the particular techniques Pinter evolved for this play. In response to Anna's confirmation that Kate was "delightful" to live with, Deeley facetiously quotes from the prewar standard of Jerome Kern, "Lovely to look at, delightful to know," which he repeats, causing Kate to ask Anna, "Did we have it?" This evokes their relationship, whatever it may have been, before Deeley, who counters by singing to Kate, "You're lovely to look at, delightful to know," reclaiming her in the equivocal suggestiveness of "to know." Unperturbed, Anna answers: "Oh we did. Yes, of course. We had them all." The double *we* is both heavily inclusive and exclusive. Thereafter, a stichomythic song battle takes place, drawing on the familiar great pop standards of the prewar era— by Jerome Kern, George Gershwin, Rogers and Hart, and others. Noel Coward remarked, famously, on the potency of popular music. The evocative melodies echoing conventional sentiment and romance might seem comic and distracting, but a powerful irony runs through as each singer covertly vies for supremacy in this unique power struggle. Consider the following in this light:

ANNA: (*singing*) The way you comb your hair . . .
DEELEY: (*singing*) On no they can't take that away from me . . .
ANNA: (*singing*) On but you're lovely, with your smile so warm. . .
DEELEY: (*singing*) I've got a woman crazy for me . . .

In a guarded few bars Deeley unwittingly ventures into lines from "These Foolish Things," only to find himself maneuvered by Anna into singing the lyrics "Oh, how the ghost of you clings." Deeley stops here with the realization that Kate has, in fact, become both ghostlike in her remoteness from him and in Anna's re-presentation of the past clinging to her.

After a significant silence Deeley launches into a long speech about his first encounter with Kate at a visit to see Carol Reed's famous film *Odd Man Out*. Pinter remarked on the combination of humor and crisis in his writing: "I agree that more often than not the speech only *seems* to be funny—the man in question is actually fighting a battle for his life."[2] In a television interview with Melvyn Bragg in 1978 Pinter cited this speech of Deeley's as an example. Anna has attempted to win over Kate by an aesthetic reclamation of the present as she recalls their sharing mutual interests, particularly in cinema, art, and poetry. Deeley attempts to subvert such pretension by coarseness and vulgarity.

In his *Odd Man Out* speech Deeley fights on two fronts. First, he presents his account as if he were shielding Kate from the lesbian ambience of two usherettes and, by implication, from Anna: "There were two usherettes standing in the foyer and one of them was stroking her breasts and the other was saying 'dirty bitch' and the one stroking her breasts was saying 'mmnnn' with a very sensual relish and smiling at her fellow usherette." Second, in his celebration of the famous postwar film Deeley makes a claim to cultural sophistication, the grounds Anna had used to exclude him earlier. But Deeley's joint claim on Kate, culminating in the statement "So it was Robert Newton who brought us together and it is only Robert Newton who can tear us apart," uses an aesthetic judgment to reinforce an emotional claim. Anna, unintimidated by the lesbian slur, undermines the latter by challenging the former: "F. J. McCormick was good too."

Deeley can only feebly counter this at first and is thus impelled into provokingly recounting their first sexual overture. Anna responds with the oft-quoted line about memory: "There are some things one remembers." This paradox offers a fascinating gloss on the psychology of memory and on the play as a whole, but its structural and dramatic primacy in its textual placement should not be lost sight of. Anna is here almost directly challenging the credibility of Deeley's suggestive erotic recall, in response to his question "What do you think?" Seizing the initiative, Anna continues with a riposte to his story of sexual acceptance, offering an account of his sexual rejection: "This man crying in our room. One night late I returned and found him sobbing, his hand over his face, sitting in the armchair, all crumpled in the armchair and Katey sitting on the bed"—an image anticipated in the very first stage directions "DEELEY *slumped in armchair, still*" (3).

Anna triumphs at the close, since in the final action the posture is reenacted: "DEELEY *starts to sob, very quietly* (69); *He walks slowly to the armchair. He sits, slumped*" (70). The emotion generated onstage is in inverse proportion to its very quietness. But, in fact, it is Kate who rejects both. Following the story of the man in the bedroom, Anna seemingly reappropriates Kate by relating that they had gone together to see *Odd Man Out.* Yet Kate signals her joint rejection of them both with a remark in which seriousness is muted by comedy. Anna declares, "And later when I found out the kind of man you were I was doubly delighted because I knew Katey had always been interested in the arts." To which Kate replies, "I was interested once in the arts, but I can't remember now which ones they were" (33). The comedy of such ludicrous improbability should not totally obscure the fact that Kate uses lack of memory to disengage herself from both Deeley and Kate in the past and present. Kate says very little until the end of the play, when echoes of Deeley and Anna are heard in her voice, but Kate's aestheticism is finer than Anna's coloratura, and the harshness of her symbolic interment is much more destructive than Deeley's aggression. In expressionistic reply to Deeley and Kate's ritualization of her bath, she recounts that she "plastered his face with dirt" (69) and comparably, with Anna: "Your face was dirty. You lay dead" (67).

In many ways the revue sketch "Night" (1969) anticipates the full-length work *Old Times*. Although it is not quoted, the sketch in effect dramatizes Maurice Chevalier and Hermione Gingold's duet "I Remember It Well," in which lovers' memories are controverted by each other. In "Night" arbitrary memory undermines the uniqueness of romantic encounter. Pinter observed that the "shared common ground" of experience is more like a "quicksand," a situation often found when negotiating the hazards of memory.[3]

In bereavement there is the memory of love, but in such a rejection as Deeley's there is the nullity of nonbeing. Deeley has had his memory obliterated by Anna and then Kate, and he is reduced to nothingness. As Anna unknowingly anticipates, "It was as if he had never been" (29). Too complex for pathos, Deeley's final loss is the closest Pinter gets to tragic experience.

No Man's Land (1975)

Francis King, the novelist, recorded how his friend L. P. Hartley had an absolute horror of "normal" servants in his Hampstead household. This and the Ortonesque notoriety of Jack Straw's Castle, a Hampstead pub, may well have coalesced in Pinter's mind after visits to Hartley to discuss the screenplay of *The Go-Between*. "Those images that yet, / Fresh images beget" may have produced Hirst, the wealthy man of letters; Spooner, the down-at-heel poet; and Briggs and Foster, the bizarre servant and secretary, all found in the Hampstead household of *No Man's Land*.

At a glance it would appear that the play offers an upper-class rerun of *The Caretaker*, fifteen years on. On being invited back from a pub to Hirst's evidently well-off household, Spooner opportunistically recognizes short- and long-term possibilities of patronage—drink and food, a job with a salary, and perhaps a home. But this is to reckon without the stakes of Briggs and Foster, who immediately grasp what is going on and embark on a blatantly sarcastic and threatening strategy of exclusion—again, an intruder, a power struggle involving place and personality, and menace and threat. But the play has much more to offer than mannerist repetition.

Following *Old Times, No Man's Land* is often linked to the memory plays, and with some justification. No-man's-land is the alcoholic stasis in which Hirst deliberately isolates himself to escape into the memory of the past, as enshrined in his totemic photograph album. But photographs are posed, generally, and often offer a front, the posture somewhat at variance with the truth. And, in effect, this provides an analogy for the disjunction between the reality of whatever the past was and its re-representation by memory, filtered by alcohol, in Hirst's case. Yet, in one remote sober part of his being, Hirst signals an equivocal doubt, which has to be quashed by assertion: "My true friends look out at me from my album. I had my world. I have it. Don't think now that it's gone I'll choose to sneer at it, to cast doubt on it, to wonder if it properly existed. No. We're talking of my youth, which can never leave me. No. It existed" (109). But the element of doubt then exacerbated by alcohol is reasserted: "It's gone. Did it exist? It's gone. It never existed. It remains" (110).

Spooner had earlier encouraged Hirst's reverie, not without a touch of literary irony: "We share something. A memory of the bucolic life." To which Hirst responds with a Tennysonian echo, "All who die unmarried, wearing the white flower of a blameless life" (93). This passage will need to be reexamined shortly, but here it should be noted how a major aspect of Pinter's structure is the calculated comic use of the deflationary story, or mock epiphany. The idea of epiphany has been considered in relation to the significance of the revue sketches. Elsewhere in poetry and prose of the twentieth century, particularly in the art of the short story, the epiphanic mode has been central to the portrayal and interpretation of experience. The epiphany is that moment or occasion when meaning is made manifest in a usually heightened experience of self-revelation, not unlike revisionary interpretations of Aristotle's "anagnorisis" which take it beyond simple "recognition" into larger insight into the nature of things.

In *No Man's Land* the mock epiphany becomes a parodic reflection on the different kinds of failure of the characters, particularly those of literary standing or aspiration, even Foster, for, as Briggs claims, "He's a poet" (129). Spooner recounts the story of his revelatory encounter with the Hungarian émigré, yet he has forgotten what was said (87–89). Pinter provides Spooner with the aesthetic conundrum of a painting, "The Whistler." The painting depicts a sentimental piscatory scene by an Amsterdam canal and includes "a man whistling under his breath" (103). Spooner asks if they would have been baffled by the title. The synesthetic incompatibility of seeing and hearing is self-defeating and thus a mark of Spooner's contempt. Yet he is hoist by his own petard since he is the fish out of water because, like the man silently whistling, he is not part of where he finds himself. Foster delays his real reply until his counter-epiphany of an "old stinking tramp, bollock naked," and gets Spooner to indirectly identify himself: "He was a con artist" (106). There are many other mock epiphanies in the play, since it is largely structured around such anecdotal re-creation and recall (for example, the stories of the Australian desert [116–17] and Bolsover Street [124–25]). But of greatest importance is Hirst's struggle to sustain an epiphanic sense of the past, though it is repeatedly shattered by his dream of the drowning man and subverted by Pinter's creation of dramatic conflict from binary tension beneath the surface structure of speech and movement.

Hirst's retreat into no-man's-land is to protect himself from loneliness and degradation in the present, with his charades of dignity and friendship and an idealized past. Furthermore, in the play as a whole Pinter also exploits formalized oppositions of language with the literary and mannered juxtaposed against the coarse and vulgar. A corollary to this is found in the opposed memories of the past. There is the Tennysonian evocation of virginity and the "bucolic" life, but in act 2 is found the "insane and corrosive sexual absolutism" (138) of Hirst's homosexual corruption and heterosexual betrayal, in a sequence that pays tribute to Noel Coward in a comically outrageous pastiche that is nevertheless, as with all Pinter's humor, finally serious.

In the temporal structure of the play act 1 opens on a summer night in which Spooner witnesses Hirst's drunken degradation as he crawls from the room, whereas act 2 opens with the apparent sobriety and order of morning and Hirst's immaculate entry, bent on revenge with his story of betrayal. Day, however, is speedily transformed by alcoholism into night, and then into a symbolic winter, when the curtains are drawn: "The subject is now winter. So it'll therefore be winter forever" (154); "It's night. . . . And will always be night" (156). As in *The Homecoming,* the source of drama is not so much in overt action and speech as in the carefully assembled counterpoint of binary oppositions in the clash of ethos and idiolect.

From the outset the dignity of Hirst's bearing contrasts absolutely with the degradation of his alcoholic collapse, when he has to crawl from the room. As Briggs says shortly after, "You'd crawl to the bottle and stuff it between your teeth," to which Hirst replies, in complete self-delusion: "No. I drink with dignity" (109). This physical aspect is complemented by something much more insidiously comic almost throughout the second act. Consider the following examples:

Hirst's interjection, "We three, never forget, are the oldest of friends" (147), in the midst of resonant obscenity insures the travesty of friendship he asserts, thereby heightening the sense of his inner solitude, just at the point of audience laughter, in spite of equivocal companionship and apparent socializing. In the midst of such friendship, loneliness; in the midst of such vulgarity, the pathos of Hirst's refinement.

Again, in act 2 Foster urges Briggs to speak to Spooner:

> BRIGGS: To him? To a pisshole collector? To a shithouse operator? To a jamrag vendor? What the fuck are you talking about? Look at him. He's a minge juice bottler, a fucking shitcake baker. What are you talking to him for?
> HIRST: Yes, yes, but he's a good man at heart. I knew him at Oxford.
> *Silence.*
> SPOONER: (*to Hirst*) Let me live with you and be your secretary.
> (150)

It is characteristic of Pinter's writing that, for all the assaulting obscenity of such language, what is going on beneath the relief of laughter provoked by Hirst and Spooner's response is something extremely subtle. Cessation of the Lord Chamberlain's censorship allowed dramatists complete freedom to explore the whole range of demotic language. In the New York run of the first production of *No Man's Land* Briggs appeared in the first act wearing a blazer with a regimental badge, which was precisely right for this kind of barrack-room pornography. Hirst's response, hilarious in its absolute contrast, evokes the socially exclusive prewar world of scholarship and learned society. After the silence in which Spooner absorbs the possibilities of Hirst's remark, in a highly mannered affectation of literary nuance, he characteristically echoes poetry with the sexual ambivalence of Marlovian pastoral.

Within this sequence vulgarity and degradation contrast with the refinement and dignity of Hirst, which has already been undermined by his earlier behavior and speech. Within the circularity of the whole play (night, day, and artificial "night") are developed the shaping oppositions of culture, literature, and love, undermined by coarseness, obscenity, and crude sex. Pinter's binarism exploits the dissonant clash of linguistic registers, and he is at his subtlest here. Spooner's echo of "Come live with me and be my love" both advertises himself and compliments Hirst, as literary men, simultaneously snubbing Foster and Briggs. Sexual suggestivity vies with wit, by which Spooner can either advance or retreat, depending on Hirst's response. But, finally, at the close of the formalized antiphony of Briggs and Foster's coda, Spooner, recognizing that Hirst acts out precisely what he wants, intones a refrain that outdoes the close of Pirandello's *Henry IV* and Sartre's *Huis Clos:* "No man's land. Which never moves, which never changes, which never grows older, but which remains forever, icy and silent" (157).

Monologue (1973)

Dramatic isolation is the central image of the short television play *Monologue,* in which a man seated on one chair addressed another as if his absent friend were there. This brief work is discussed here in order to introduce the full-length work *Betrayal* (1978). *Monologue* offers in epitome, and brings out in high relief, a major concern of Pinter's work which has been partly obscured by the categories "comedy of menace" and "memory plays"—namely, friendship and betrayal.[4] The title *Betrayal* speaks for itself. In *Monologue* the unnamed speaker asks, "Who was your best mate, who was your truest mate?" (276), and bemoans the situation "as if our sporting and intellectual life never was" (297). Pinter is particularly drawn to rivalry as a form of power struggle within friendship, and this takes two forms, one of which, rivalry in love, is entirely predictable. "Now you're going to say you loved her soul and I loved her body. . . . But I'll tell you one thing you don't know. She loved my soul. It was my soul she loved" (277), the speaker claims.

The other all-pervasive form of rivalry is that of competitive sport and games.[5] In his youth Pinter held his school's record for running 100 and 200 yards, he was a fine footballer, and he has always acknowledged sharing one of the most intense passions of Englishness—cricket. *Monologue* opens thus: "I think I'll nip down to the games room. Stretch my legs. Have a game of ping pong. What about you? Fancy a game? How would you like a categorical thrashing?" (275). Rivalry in sport and love is central in *The Basement, Accident,* and *The Go-Between,* to which *Monologue* is a kind of epilogue, while from this point of view it also becomes a prelude for *Betrayal.*

Betrayal (1978)

The title *Betrayal* made emphatic what had always been a dramatic concern in almost all of Pinter's stage and screen work. "Themes madam, nay I know not themes" was said to be Kenneth Tynan's response to a lady who asked for the main themes of *Hamlet*. The elucidation of "themes" is now largely discredited in the rarefied hothouse of late twentieth-century critical theory, since such practice could often lead to naive and reductive crudities. Yet thematic criticism can perform a function still, particularly where critical discourse is tied to repeated paradigms, which was the case in early Pinter criticism, in which menace, power, subservience, verification, and other leading concerns were endlessly discussed. Pinter himself felt no qualms when speaking of "the major themes" of Proust in the introduction to *The Proust Screenplay* (vii). Friendship and betrayal are "major themes" in Pinter's work, yet in recent years critical theory has evolved in such as way as to provide a more discriminating perspective on this issue. In the development of gender studies from that of feminism we have an analytic tool to reassess a play such as *Betrayal* (if not a great deal of Pinter's work) in terms of *maleness*.

Betrayal was immediately successful, with its relative realism and subject—adultery among the London literati—which seemed a familiar addition, along with something like Tom Stoppard's *The Real Thing* (1982), to fiction and theater of the period, in spite of the innovative backward time structure. *Betrayal* appears to be a 1970s comedy of manners concerned with intrigue, betrayal, and hypocrisy. Pinter delights in portraying domestic surfaces, but there is considerably more to the play than that. First, the unusual structure needs to be outlined. The play is divided into nine scenes. In the first, set in 1977, Jerry meets up with Emma, his best friend's wife, with whom he had had an affair for seven years, which ended two years previously. She announces that her marriage to Robert is over and that he has been told of the affair. Scene 2 takes place later the same evening with Robert going to Jerry's house, where he explains that Emma actually told him of the affair four years earlier. Scene 3 begins the backward movement and is in Jerry and Emma's love nest, a rented flat, in 1975, and depicts the desultory end of their now passionless affair. The backward movement is continued in scene 4, in 1974, with Robert, Emma, and Jerry debating the merits of a contemporary novel and the game of squash. More dramatically, in scene 5, with Robert and Emma on holiday in Venice in 1973, the adultery is confessed. The next scene actually moves forward to later in 1973, with Emma and Jerry resuming their liaison after the Venice holiday. The forward movement continues in scene 7, later in 1973, again, with Robert and Jerry lunching in a restaurant. Scene 8 resumes the backward movement with the establishment of the love flat in 1971, and scene 9 ends at the beginning, with Jerry's first pass at Emma in 1968 at a party, with her and Robert as hosts.

One fundamental irony needs to be stressed. Whenever Robert appears in the play he is aware of Jerry and Emma's betrayal, except for the last scene, which closes on this exchange:

> JERRY: I speak as your oldest friend. Your best man.
> ROBERT: You are, actually.

> (272)

Thus, apart from this, whenever he appears, Robert is under the strain of multiple betrayal—of friendship, of marriage, and of family—and this should influence critical appraisal of his dialogue. Evasion of communication is explored here in a psychologically involved form. Why did Robert never confront Jerry with the knowledge of betrayal as soon as he knew of it? *Betrayal* has a complex dimension in the implicit exploration of the psychology of friendship as a specific condition of maleness. Gender studies recognizes biological sexuality deriving from nature but directs its attention to the cultural formation of gender behavior—"masculinity" and "femininity"—as socially determined.

At the heart of the play Pinter dramatizes the conflict between the values of friendship and faithfulness. In terms of gender this is specifically between the bonds of male friendship and the oaths of marital fidelity Jerry and Robert have made to their wives. For years Jerry has carried on the affair while maintaining friendship, seemingly without any sense of betrayal. At first, on learning of Emma's admission, Jerry separates betrayal of friendship from disclosure of adultery and shows no sense of his responsibility in inaugurating the affair. But, when he finds out that Emma's confession was made four years ago, he is more dismayed by Robert's unfaithfulness as a friend in not facing him than with Emma's duplicity or his own exposure.

Something more complex than hypocrisy is at work here. When he sees Robert in act 2 Jerry says: "I thought I was going to go mad. . . . After all, you and me" (184–85), as if their friendship had been endangered, rather than Robert and Emma's marriage finished. To Jerry the primacy of maleness reciprocated in friendship must be inviolable, whereas the lesser bonds of male-female relationships are naturally vulnerable. In scene 4 Pinter embarks on a long-drawn-out comic exchange between Robert and Jerry on the apparently greater anxiety of "boy babies" and their crying in comparison with "girl babies." Since the experience between the sexes in babyhood is mutual, no logic can support the proposition, so the argument develops circularly by completely begging the question. But logic is not at issue here, for behind the fallacy both Robert and Jerry are agreeing on the greater sensitivity of maleness from birth. This scene is set in 1974, in the year following Robert's learning of the betrayal in Venice. As the scene progresses with discussion of Casey's latest novel and its relative honesty or dishonesty in representing marital breakdown, text and subtext draw closer and closer until, passing into the possibility of a game of squash and Emma's offering to take them to lunch afterward, Robert turns on her with a seriocomic speech, which is part of Pinter's formalized pattern of very brief dialogue exchange just occasionally halted by a long speech that centers the subtextual concerns of the play. Hence the full speech is given here:

> Well, to be brutally honest, we wouldn't actually want a woman around, would we, Jerry? I mean a game of squash isn't simply a game of squash, it's rather more than that. You see, first there's the game. And then there's the shower. And then there's the pint. And then there's lunch. After all, you've been at it. You've had your battle. What you want is your pint and your lunch. You really don't want a woman buying you lunch. You don't actually want a woman within a mile of the place, any of the places, really. You don't want her in the squash court, you don't want her in the shower, or the pub, or the restaurant. You see, at lunch you want to talk about squash, or cricket, or books, or even women, with your friend, and be able to warm to your theme without fear of improper interruption. That's what it's all about. What do you think, Jerry? (213–14)

Robert evokes the exclusive world of masculinity: athletic, competitive, and asexual, unless the view is taken that such a position is necessarily homosexual, however sublimated. The three words *heterosexual, homosexual,* and *bisexual* are hardly adequate for the infinite gradations of human sexual relationships. In Jerry's case his life has been one of a kind of complementary adulation for Robert. Like the speaker and friend in *Monologue,* and Stott and Law in *The Basement,* Robert and Jerry shared sporting and intellectual interests. Both were editors of university poetry magazines, both marrying and having a boy and a girl, both holidaying in Venice, both in the book world complementing each other as agent and publisher. As Robert mockingly says to Emma: "I've always liked Jerry. To be honest, I've always liked him rather more than I've liked you. Maybe I should have had an affair with him myself" (229). Because Jerry believes that male friendship is separate in its inviolability, it is of a different order than sexual relationship—unless the alternative view is taken, that in loving Emma he has taken the last step possible toward closeness to Robert, excluding actual homosexuality. Whichever emphasis is made, a gender reading has considerably greater depth than an unalloyed moralistic response.

One specific example will bring out the peculiar psychology of male friendship. In scene 5, precisely when Robert becomes aware of Jerry's betrayal, he recalls that, as student editors, they exchanged long letters about such figures as W. B. Yeats. There and then, seeking solitude, Robert goes to Torcello, leaving Emma behind, but takes a copy of Yeats's poetry, although the poet has just been associated with Jerry and friendship. When they return from Venice he mentions his reading of Yeats on

Torcello to Jerry, at lunch, in scene 7. Four years later, in the
confrontation over betrayal and divorce, Jerry says that he is
reading Yeats and adds, "You read Yeats on Torcello once" (193).
It would appear, taking this memory as indicative, that Jerry's
whole adult life has been influenced by the idea and fact of Robert and friendship. Yet, paradoxically, it is Jerry who betrays himself as friend, in the chain of cause and effect which goes back
to 1968.

When precisely Robert started his affairs is never made clear,
but there are no indications that it was before Emma's confession. In the isolation, suffering, and silence behind the insouci-
ant mask put on by Daniel Massey, the creator of the role, Robert
hung on to the idea of friendship, knowing of Jerry's betrayal,
while Jerry persisted in believing that in the midst of subterfuge
and secrecy friendship still obtained. That anomaly is the measure of the moral distance between them. If Jerry's behavior has
to be seen ultimately as something peculiar, if not perverse, then
Robert's forbearance takes on a kind of generosity in his refusal
to condemn friendship. But such a paradoxical situation is emotionally corrosive, and the man who had gladly acknowledged
his "oldest friend" and "best man" ends by saying to that same
person, "You don't seem to understand that I don't give a shit
about any of this" (189).

Other Places (1982)

Three shorter plays, *Family Voices* (1981), *Victoria Station*
(1982), and *A Kind of Alaska* (1982), were performed and published together under the title *Other Places.*

Family Voices is almost an epitome of postmodernism, though it could be argued that much of Pinter's writing from the very beginning anticipates this formulation of contemporary theory. Postmodernism is something of a theoretical ragbag, drawing on very diverse materials, and, if some of the leading characteristics that arise in discussion are named, it is immediately possible to discern their relevance to Pinter's writing: the mixture of popular and high art forms, subversion of convention, absurdist parody, indeterminacy and excess, disorientation of the reader-auditor. All of these are true of *The Birthday Party.* Postmodernism in part derives its impetus from both a critique of the positivist basis of mimetic realism in the "classic" realist novel of the nineteenth century and, conversely, from a critique of the modernist absorption of reality into the transcendence of art, as in Joyce's *Ulysses.*

In *Family Voices,* conceived originally for radio production, a young man, Voice 1, having left home, recounts his life as a lodger in the bizarre residence of the Withers family. His mother, Voice 2, in plaintive vacillation, wonders where, and how, he is. The father, Voice 3, speaks from the grave. *Family Voices* is neither an epistle nor a monologue and does not settle comfortably into any conventional radio work. Is the son, indeed, a homosexual prostitute, as his mother charges at one point or merely an innocent abroad? His epicene language could be taken either way. He claims he got drunk, identifies himself as a teetotaler, yet recounts drinking sessions with Mrs. Withers. Language varies from rococo excess (in praise of currant buns) to demotic idiolect ("no shit from that quarter" [295]). Attitudes and statements become self-canceling. The son is happy and unhappy; he needs his mother then no longer does. The mother yearns for her son yet curses him. The father is dead and is not dead; he speaks from the grave and concludes by denying the possibility of speaking from the grave. Yet placing *Family Voices* within the canon of Pinter's work makes clear once more the reverse and obverse of a lifelong fascination, the subjection of normalcy to the bizarre. "What's normal?" Deeley asks in *Old Times* (11).

In fact, the three plays of *Other Places* all concern different kinds of the bizarre. *Victoria Station* draws attention to Pinter's dramatic use of London topography. When recently depositing sixty boxes of his manuscripts with the British Library in London, the playwright remarked, "I was born in London, you know." Pinter cleverly exploits the topographical character and distance between the railway station and Crystal Palace to parallel the mental and social positions of the minicab driver and his controller. The night view from the southern perimeter heights of Crystal Palace to the center of London and Victoria Station reflects the amorphous divide between them. The lonely driver has found the love of his life; the controller seems to be half-crazed with loneliness and the impossibility of getting a message through. Throughout his work Pinter has used London topography with great specificity, perhaps nowhere more so than in the commemorative poem written ten years after the death of his schooldays mentor, "Joseph Brearley 1909–1977 (Teacher of English)."[6] Here Pinter parallels the solidity of the east London locale of his youth with the shadowy epiphenomenon of memory, confounding absence and presence, shifting emotion into the remote emptiness of deserted nighttime districts.

Nothing could be more bizarre than the situation in *A Kind of Alaska,* yet it was a grotesque widespread reality of earlier this century which history preferred to forget until reminded by

Dr. Oliver Sacks's account of the victims of *encephalitis lethargica,* a sleeping sickness, in his book *Awakenings* (1973). Discovery of the drug L-dopa meant that after some thirty-odd years in a largely comatose state victims were reawakened into life. Recently, a successful film with the same title was made. Pinter's full reaction to Sacks's book is not on record, but it must have been something of a shock, since it reflects in case histories much that is relevant to his work. Here, indeed, was a no-man's-land between sleep and waking, between life and death—a reverse tragedy, in which life is denied and death preempted. Isolation in space and time is a major aspect of Pinter's oeuvre. In Sacks's book it was found in a literal, ironic sense, for the awakened victims had no actual present, only a past historically distant but still immediately present for them. In middle-aged bodies were eternal youths exiled amid the living ghosts of memory. Apart from fingers flickering across the face of Deborah, a victim, Pinter only took the general situation from the book for *A Kind of Alaska.*

From the moment of Deborah's awakening Pinter recognized that this reality must appear to speak for itself with minimal stylization or structural innovation, as an expression of his propriety and respect. The middle-aged Deborah speaks for her sixteen-year-old self, in turn sophisticated and pedestrian, childish and worldly, with anecdote and incident, of family and friends around "Townley Street." The audience is compromised by Deborah's humor with the growing realization that, for all the numbing particularity of her experience, described by Dr. Hornby, her self-sacrificing physician, as "a kind of Alaska" (336), it bears the shocking possibility of an analogue for any individual life.

Such arresting simplicity, with such powerful reverberations, led to something unique in Pinter's career—the unanimous critical acknowledgment that here was a masterpiece, without demur.

As part of the celebrations for Pinter's sixtieth birthday, BBC radio put on a production of *A Kind of Alaska,* with Pinter himself as Dr. Hornby. This brought out most strikingly a dimension of further analogical significance—that for all its verisimilitude the play symbolized Pinter's creative process. Pinter-as-Hornby patiently nurturing the sleeping victim for as long as it took, until revivified, was like an image of the artist waiting upon the inscrutable workings of the creative imagination to demand independent life. From this point of view Deborah's fate reflects that of all humanity, ineluctably subjected to space, time, and memory.

Notes

1. "Writing for the Theatre," *Plays One* (London: Faber, 1991), xiii.

2. "Harold Pinter: An Interview" (with Lawrence Bensky), in *Pinter: A Collection of Critical Essays,* edited by Arthur Ganz (Englewood Cliffs, N.J.: Prentice-Hall, 1972), 31.

3. "Writing for the Theatre," x.

4. See Ronald Knowles, "Friendship and Betrayal in the Plays of Harold Pinter," *Long Room* nos. 28–29 (1984).

5. See Guido Almansi and Simon Henderson, *Harold Pinter* (London and New York: Methuen, 1983).

6. *Collected Poems and Prose* (London: Faber, 1991), 46.

CHAPTER SEVEN

Screenplays, 1971–93:
From *The Go-Between* to *The Trial*

The Go-Between (1971)

With L. P. Hartley's novel of 1953, Pinter and Joseph Losey returned to the subject of class consciousness, sexuality, and Englishness, but here in a pronounced form, since the fiction is set in 1900, at the close of the Victorian period. In the setting of country house aristocratic munificence are all the finely graded class differentials, from the peripheral laboring classes to local tenant farmers, and in the great house itself is the double hierarchy of servants and masters, at the apex of which sits the squire, Mr. Maudsley, and his guest Lord Trimingham.

The film exploits two perspectives, that of young Leo Colston as he visits the wealthy estate of his school friend Marcus's family and, briefly, the flash-forwards to the aged Leo revisiting after a lifetime. In the long hot summer of 1900 the youthful Leo, though from a not-too-well-off middle-class background, basks in privileged sunshine, while the brief flash-forwards develop a remarkably painful poignancy, with the bowed older figure in rain-darkened sadness. In filming, Losey took one item of natural history from Hartley's novel, but, what must have been to his great delight, he found another on arriving at the location.

"Atropa belladonna" twelve-year-old Leo insists on as the taxonomically correct name for the deadly nightshade that he discovers in the grounds of Brandham Hall, the country seat of his aristocratic school friend. "Every part of it is poison" (290), he adds, suggesting interpretative symbolic qualities lacking in *Accident*. The dialogue of *Accident* is almost wholly banal and deliberately so. The unspoken drama remains within the characters, to be hinted at by the suggestibility of the camera, not declared by language or mediated by symbol. *Atropa* comes from Atropos, one of the three fates, who cut the thread of life; *belladonna* means "beautiful lady." Young Leo becomes the go-between for the lovers, Marian, Marcus's beautiful sister, and Ted Burgess, a local tenant farmer. Marian is "atropa belladonna" for both Leo and Ted. The thread of life is cut for Ted when he shoots himself after their affair is discovered. Leo's life is metaphorically cut short, since the traumatic experience of the adolescent discovery of illicit copulation emotionally withers him. Marian tells the sixty-year-old Leo, whose return provides a narrative frame, "You're all dried up inside" (360), like the deadly nightshade he finally uprooted as a youth.

Losey had the good fortune to find, and the genius to use, a huge tree in the grounds of the country estate location. This ancient tree had become so unwieldy and overgrown that its massive contorted branches had become far too heavy for it, and they had to be supported by a large number of props. Losey realized the rich possibilities of this visual image. Within the context of the narrative, viewed from below, the contorted branches were sexually suggestive of interlocking limbs. As an emblem, the contortions evoked the social and moral contortions of the prohibited liaison. Leo seeks from the evasive Ted exactly what is meant by the intimacy of "spooning" (322), and the tree comes to suggest Leo's own tree of knowledge. The carnal discovery that he is exposed to by Marian's avenging mother leads to his "fall"—an immediate nervous breakdown and a lifetime of emotional privation. Finally, in an almost heraldic sense the tree is, indeed, a family tree propped up by a class system doomed not to survive the First World War. In the course of Leo's stay in the record-breaking hot summer, testified by the thermometer hanging from the tree, with images of harvest and a brief discussion of the army, Pinter and Losey just hint at what is made explicit in Hartley's novel, when Marian tells Leo of those who fell in the Great War.

The details touched on here indicate the extraordinary visual richness of a sequence such as that when Losey's camera, from above the tree, tracks Leo as he makes his way to destroy the deadly nightshade. Leo's subsequent incantation in his magic ritual of destruction succinctly compresses the meaning of a whole sequence in Pinter's line "Delenda, delenda, delenda" (353). As Hartley hints, Leo probably derives his spell from Cato's refrain, "Delenda est Carthago" (Carthage must be destroyed). In one of Pinter's most subtle and poignant screen directions, not indicated in the novel, the significance of natural in relation to human history—the tree, the war, a whole era—is encapsulated at the close as the aging Leo catches a final glimpse of Brandham Hall: "*The elms have been cut down*" (367).

SCREENPLAYS, 1971–93

The Proust Screenplay (1972)

Marcel Proust's monumental *A la recherche du temps perdu*—or *The Remembrance of Things Past,* as it is known in English—is devoted to the labyrinthine exploration of involuntary memory. In 1972 and 1973 Pinter worked with Joseph Losey and Barbara Bray on a screenplay, a year that the dramatist then considered the "best working year" of his life.[1] Funds were not found for production, and with the death of Losey it seems unlikely that the film will be made.

The printed screenplay remains as one of the most fascinating works by Pinter. By any standard what is achieved is remarkable. To take the gigantic work built largely around the introspection of its writer-hero Marcel and turn it into a visual medium is impressive, but the visual cue was there to be found in Proust as well as the possibilities of sound. Pinter's introduction tells us "that the architecture of the film should be based on two main and contrasting principles: one a movement, chiefly narrative, towards disillusion, and the other, more intermittent, towards revelation, rising to where time that was lost is found, and fixed forever in art."[2]

Pinter resists the danger of excessive voice-over and exploits cinematic experience by stressing image and sound: Vermeer's view of Delft, the garden gate bell at Cambray, the steeples at Martinville, and Vinteuil's music. The technique that Pinter develops to accommodate such variety is that of serial montage. Central to Proust's concern with involuntary memory was the evocation upon tasting the little madeleine in the first volume,

Swann's Way. This is probably one of the most famous passages in the work, yet Pinter dropped it. It is not difficult to see why: sight and sound could be exploited, but taste was impossible. For Pinter's approach consider the following sequence. The young Marcel visiting Balbec with his grandmother feels lonely and knocks three times on the wall separating their rooms. The knock is answered three times, and she lovingly appears. Later in Balbec, after his grandmother's demise, the older Marcel bends to unbutton his shoes, and the intromission of memory takes place, in close-up: "*His face*" is "*overcome with grief. On the soundtrack, three knocks are heard on the wall*" (see 35–36, 87–88).

What the screen realization of such moments as the Verdurin's party, at which the rediscovered Vinteuil septet is played, would be like remains speculative. In the screenplay shots 315–29 (130–31) move from the almost wholly decadent fin de siècle audience to Marcel's joyousness at the climax of the music, in which the dutiful applause is heard against shots of the Vermeer and a flash of the steeples, Marcel's inner world of artistic epiphany triumphing over the refined crassness around him. Having been steeped in the Proustian world of literary art, memory, and sexual ambivalence for a year, it is not surprising that Pinter worked through these concerns in his next full-length work, *No Man's Land,* the following year.

The Last Tycoon (1977)

F. Scott Fitzgerald's death in 1940 left *The Last Tycoon* both unfinished and unrevised. The novel is set in Hollywood of the

1930s, with its leading figure, Monroe Stahr, modeled on that of producer Irving Thalberg. In the screenplay Pinter immediately dispensed with the first-person narrator, as he did in *The Servant,* and seized on the metafilmic possibilities that Fitzgerald had indicated as the core of his examination of reality, representation, and illusion. In ironic reflexivity and 1930s pop culture Fitzgerald was ahead of his time, since these are now regarded as aspects of postmodernism. Moreover, the concept that pop images shape reality has grown increasing apparent in the movement from a literary to a visual culture during the course of the century.

In the opening sequence of the film Pinter added material not found in Fitzgerald. A black-and-white restaurant scene erupts into a gangland slaying after the tip-off signal of a swaying lamp. With a cut to a projection room, in color, Stahr's criticism of the signal as "too obvious" is heard (193). Similarly, Stahr continues by moving to criticism of a romantic shot of lovers by the sea. These clear representations of cinematic illusion will become some sort of reality—of crime, of passion—for the audience. Then the issue of illusion and reality is complicated by a studio tour guide, with a party, observing the dressing room of Stahr's film star wife, Minna Davis, in which she died. The reality of the room becomes a melodrama as an exhibit, with the tourist party as audience, for which Minna Davies's death acted out another, final role. Past actuality makes illusion more "real" as the cinematic imagination of the visitors reenacts and replays a celluloid death. Further shots develop this self-reflexive mode, including the guide's explanation of how the illusion of the San Francisco earthquake was achieved. A real earthquake then takes place, tremors creating an artificial river, which destroys various sets. Art, illusion, and reality are completely confounded in a mock surrealism: the giant head of Siva floats along with two women clinging to it for safety, while film workers look laconically on, commenting, "De Mille needs that head next week" (203).

Monroe Stahr, the successful creator of romantic illusions, is seen as a hardheaded businessman-manager-technician adeptly handling the personal and industrial problems of film production (until he gets uncharacteristically drunk). His expertise even extends to demonstrating how to write screenplays for inept writers, and Pinter immediately seized on it both as central for the film and as a means to resolve the problem of the unfinished novel. Before Boxley, an English writer, Stahr enacts with mime and stage directions the story of a girl who enters and places various items on a table then proceeds to burn gloves in a stove as she protests to a sudden phone caller: "I've never owned a pair of black gloves in my life." It becomes apparent that she is being watched all the time by a man. "What happened?" Boxley asks. "I don't know. I was just making pictures" (229), Stahr replies.

The otherwise pragmatic film mogul has glimpsed, on the floating head of Siva, a girl, Kathleen, who resembles his dead wife, thus revealing a passionate side to him, deeply susceptible to love. Ironically, though drawn into a relationship and sympathetic to Stahr, Kathleen is not susceptible to his power as movie magnate or lover, and she pragmatically marries someone else. Kathleen is unmoved by movies. "Movies are necessary" to people; "I give them what they need," Stahr says. "What you need" (239), Kathleen replies. Finally ousted in a boardroom coup, Stahr repeats his earlier scenario to Boxley, which becomes a voice-over, while Kathleen is seen fulfilling the mimed actions as she burns his letter, her new husband looking on. Effectively rejected, the lovelorn Stahr is truly compromised by his own sophistication. Fiction becomes fact, but love is neither subverted nor vindicated; rather, it is made paradoxical. Did Stahr love Kathleen for herself, or was their lovemaking a reenactment of his old passion, as is hinted, and Kathleen thus an unwitting actress? These metafilmic ambiguities of art and life to some degree prepared Pinter for the problems of the screenplay for *The French Lieutenant's Woman* (1981).

Langrishe, Go Down (1978)

At the beginning of *Langrishe, Go Down* a torn cinema poster advertises "*Forbidden Heaven. . . . Romance and pathos among four human derelicts*" (117), an ironic contrast with what follows in Aidan Higgins's prizewinning novel of 1966, which combines a Joycean delicacy of style and a Chekhovian sense of the comitragic in its depiction of the decline of a landowning Anglo-Irish family of three sisters on a decaying estate. The film is set in the countryside of 1938, where Helen, Lily, and Imogen Langrishe face middle-aged spinsterhood and the necessary sale of the house. For Helen and Lily stoicism and eccentricity fortify their isolation amid the plaintive strains of John McCormack and Galli-Curci, but Imogen's emptiness is reflected in empty bottles and in the memory of her one passionate affair at the beginning of the decade.

Otto Beck, a thirty-five-year-old German doctoral student
of philosophy and philology and part-time polymath, takes up
temporary residence in a lodge on the estate in order to pursue
comparative study of Irish mythology. Otto's Teutonic intellectuality is devoted to taking words apart. He does not see or care
that, in his love affair with Imogen, her being is resolved into
elemental passion but cannot be put back together again when
his attentions are redirected elsewhere. Indifferently aware of
himself as a natural parasite, he feeds on the formerly well-to-
do Langrishe household. The predominant cinematic techniques
used are flashback and voice-over, but not just as a convention.
One of the subtleties of David Jones's direction and Pinter's
screenplay derives from reflecting how this brief romantic fulfillment of the past comes to dominate the present, not just of
Imogen but of all three.

Flashbacks return to the inauguration, progress, and decline
of the affair, but voice-overs occurring particularly with scenes
including the sisters imply memory for all three, as if they heard
the words of Otto since each was aware of what was taking place.
This vicariousness takes on a comitragic dimension, when it is
revealed that Helen has been secretly reading Imogen's stack of
unposted love letters, their muted love poetry—"I am no good
without you. (*Pause.*) Your lovely body. (*Pause.*) Love of all my
life and all my senses" (122)—subjected to her "*mild scepti-
cism.*"

As her letters painfully reveal, Imogen's tragedy was the
one-sidedness of the affair. She obviously achieved a love that
was real and not just the imaginative compensation of subsequent years. That the love was not mutual is brought out by the

screenplay, which dwells on the social and physical awkward-ness of love encounters rather than passionate ecstasy. Otto's selfishness and intellectual arrogance are apparent in every scene, but perhaps a small detail says it all. Prompted by Imogen from his egotism, he acknowledges: "Yes. I have you indeed. A great solace" (160). Shortly after, accused by Imogen of stealing some apples, Otto replies, "Even you must appreciate that after twelve hours of abstinence the lower intestine stands severely in need of solace" (167). For Otto sex and sustenance are paralleled in the necessary gratification of bodily needs. Imogen's love is placed strongly in an antiromantic context of peasant life stressed in the opening, in contrast to John McCormack's "I hear you calling me" and the first line of male dialogue, overheard on the bus bringing Helen back from consultation over the estate with a solicitor—"You'll be the right ram when you get started" (112).

Yet, when the headlines of Imogen's paper are glimpsed, at the close, with news of the Germany-Austrian Anschluss and the spread of nazism, a darker political element intrudes. Otto had earlier shown evidence of fascist eugenics propaganda—"Irish women are so pure and clean . . . that great purity" (115)—and his greatest preference would be to return to Germany to study "phenomenological investigations" under Heidegger (the senior German professor who kept his post, supporting Hitler and the purging of Jewish academics). As he tells Imogen this, he coldly and calmly recounts the story of a friend's suicide at-tempt and proceeds to cut a wasp in half with a pair of scissors, which is shown in close-up (shot 283). But these larger political reverberations are kept implicit. Where Otto is or what he is do-ing is not known. As with Beth and Duff in *Landscape,* what

Otto has become in Imogen's mind is suggested by the final shots of her once more reading, "*her lips moving silently*" (190), her unposted letters.

The French Lieutenant's Woman (1981)

John Fowles presents a Victorian novel concerning the encounter between Charles Smithson, an upper-class paleontologist, and Sarah Woodruff, a woman apparently abandoned by her French lover. Interspersed throughout the story are quotations from, and Fowles's reflections on, the evolutionary theory and sociology of Darwin and Marx. Chapter captions provide a small anthology of Victorian values. In addition Fowles uses both Victorian statistics and contemporary thought for what becomes a meditation on history and cultural values. Nineteenth-century convention and authority is contrasted with the relative choice and freedom of the late twentieth century. Famously, in postmodernist style, the novel offers two endings: romantic union or antiromantic separation. Pinter's solution for the various problems was to accept that film could not accommodate the discursive intellectual element. With acute simplicity Pinter saw the possibilities of a metafilmic, film-within-a-film mode. Contrasts between the nineteenth and twentieth centuries could be suggested here with the parallelism of the actors playing Charles and Sarah having a casual affair during the course of the film's production. This choice, "a brilliant metaphor" for the novel, as Fowles called it, automatically gave expression to the novelist's preoccupation with Victorians constrained to fulfill certain roles and to enact social identity publicly.

Paradoxically, Sarah enacts the role of the fallen woman abandoned by her French lover, even though it transpires that seduction never took place. The French lieutenant acted the genuine lover but, as Sarah discovered, was no more than an ordinary philanderer. Sarah publicly marginalizes herself by her demonstrative self-ostracization, treading the sea-swept cob of Lyme Regis, the setting for the film. In contrast, Charles enacts his multiple roles of gentleman-scientist, master, and suitor for the hand of Ernestina, a tea merchant's daughter. In the novel Charles's telescope and his scientific work take on a metaphorical significance, as Fowles brings the nineteenth century into focus, observing the individual within the stratification of society. Indeed, the geological meaning of unconformity—a breach of continuity in the direction of rock strata—provides an apt metaphor for Sarah and Charles's relationship: her existential persistence in the negative choice of rejecting society and her revenge-like entrapment of Charles and Charles's onset of sociably unacceptable passion, the reverse of his study of fossils.

Pinter's technique is to parallel the two affairs as indicative of their respective societies, thereby each reflecting the limitations of the other, Victorian constraint and twentieth-century license. One example will bring this out. In the conservatory of Ernestina's home Charles proposes under *"an overhanging branch,"* which acts as substitute mistletoe, and *"they kiss chastely"* (sc. 16, p. 8). The following scene cuts to a hotel room in the "present" of 1979. Screen directions are as follows: *"A man and a woman in bed asleep. It is at once clear that they are the man and the woman playing* CHARLES *and* SARAH, *but we do not immediately appreciate that the time is the present then a telephone rings."* Given the situations of actors and characters (the actor has a wife, the actress a French boyfriend) and their contrast in language (formality contrasted with casual minimalism), the scenes could not be more opposed. Part of the technique here is proleptic, to anticipate what will take place when Charles sleeps with Sarah. Once this direction was taken the resolution of the two endings presented itself: eventual idyllic union for Charles and Sarah, whereas the actress Anna chooses to go off with her boyfriend and finish the affair as the film draws to completion, and the actor Mike duplicating the acting of Charles as he shouts from the window at the departing Anna—"Sarah!" (104).

Victory **(1982)**

"No man is an island complete unto himself"—Donne's famous line might well stand as epigraph for Pinter's screenplay from Conrad's novel of 1915. Nothing could seem more remote from Pinter's work than the setting for the film, the exotic orientalism of Surabaya and an island in the Java Sea. Yet there is a link, as Donne's line intimates. In many of Pinter's plays there is a sense in which the various rooms and characters are like islands—cut off in metaphorical terms and emotionally or morally on a periphery of life and being (*Monologue, Landscape,* and *Silence,* for example).

Conrad knew Villiers de L'Isle Adam's famous play *Axël* (1894) and deliberately gave the first name Axël to his hero, Heyst, in *Victory.* The most notorious line from the play is: "As for living our servants will do that for us," and this is self-consciously picked up and echoed in Pinter's screenplay, when Heyst declares: "I have lived a life of hard indifference. . . . No aims, no attachments, no friends, no acts. I leave all that to others. Let *them* live, as they call it" (189). On his father's deathbed Heyst, seeking "guidance," inherited a strange, gnomic valediction: "Look on. Make no sound" (216). And his father's portrait still looks on silently in the main room of his bungalow in his island solitude. Schopenhaurian pessimism, contempt for the world, and aloofness from the blind, rapacious, and irrational will that underlies existence are his legacy.

Heyst lives alone with a native manservant after the failure of a mining enterprise and the death of his business partner. Staying at the Schomberg Hotel while visiting Surabaya, he witnesses the abusive treatment meted out to a young English girl, Lena, who is a member of a touring orchestra. Angered, he offers to rescue her. He has "looked on," but against his father's advice he has done something. This the beginning of both his tragedy and his "victory." With Lena, Heyst goes from animal arousal and forced sex to the tenderness of familiar intimacy encouraged by Lena's young and open gratitude, affection, and love: "You should try to love me," she says. "You should try to love me as people do love each other when it is to be forever" (197).

Schomberg, the lecherous hotelier, whose advances Lena had rejected, seeks revenge and takes advantage of Jones and Ricardo's arrival, along with their servant, Pedro. Christopher Hudgins draws a comparison between Jones, Ricardo, and Heyst and Goldberg, McCann, and Stanley.[3] They seem to be criminal opportunists and professional gamblers, any sort of crime providing funds for cards and dice. Jones is a self-conscious English gentleman, Ricardo a passionate Latin, with Pedro as a native punching bag for their natural brutality, sadism, and repression. As characters, they are like a cross between Dickens and the early Brecht, as filmed by John Huston. (Pinter worked with Richard Lester, the director, but the film has never been made.)

Schomberg sets Jones and Ricardo on the trail of Heyst's supposedly hidden wealth. At their arrival on the island Heyst and Lena sense their ulterior motives, though Heyst feels incapable of physical retaliation because of his Olympian detachment and superiority to taking action, inherited from his father. When Ricardo discovers Lena he immediately surrenders to her in sensual abandon. She accedes to his overtures, knowing that it is the only way to get his concealed knife and thus enable her to prove her love for Heyst and offer him the means of self-vindication. It seems that Conrad had a Schopenhauerian view of Jones and Ricardo. In the novel Jones announces to Heyst, "I am the world itself, come to pay you a visit."[4] He and Ricardo together embody the brutal and rapacious Will of Schopenhauer's anti-Enlightenment philosophy.

Creeping up on the amorous Ricardo and oblivious to Lena's strategy, Jones is made to challenge Heyst's father's philosophy directly: "Look on. Make no sound. Mud souls, obscene. Mud bodies" (223), he says. It is hinted earlier that Jones is some kind of ascetic homosexual. He accidentally shoots Lena and then deliberately finishes off Ricardo, while Heyst recognizes Lena's sacrifice, her belief in him, and her faith in their love. Heyst makes the supreme gesture and creates a funeral pyre of the house, which consumes them both—a final, tragic, pagan affirmation.

SCREENPLAYS, 1971–93

Turtle Diary (1985)

Russell Hoban's novel (1975) about the abduction of turtles from London Zoo and their release into the ocean, with a gentle romance on the way, would seem to be about as far away from a Pinter play as you could get. Yet at the heart of the story there is something central to Pinter's work.

In the film Neaera, a successful children's writer, and William, a bookshop assistant, get to know each other through a common wish to free thirty-year-old turtles from their aquarium and to release them in Cornwall, from which they can fulfill their natural freedom in the mystery of their journey to Ascension Island. George Fairburn is the aquarium keeper, who willingly helps and falls for Neaera in the process. As the plot gets under way, so William's cordial affair with a colleague, Harriet, blooms. The allegorical implications of Hoban's novel are plain enough: individuals should resist life becoming confined to an aquarium and seek the natural freedom of the ocean. "They're in prison," Neaera says; "They're not alone in that" (119), William replies. Pinter's gentle and benign screenplay seems surprisingly atypical until, toward the close, the fate of Miss Neap is revealed.

Miss Neap, a middle-aged spinster who has a bed-sit on the same premises as William, encountered casually in the film, is found hanged with the Book of Common Prayer open at "For the Burial of the Dead at Sea," alongside instructions for her paid-up cremation in which she requests no service and no mourners. In despair's boundless sea the neap is the lowest tide, while with hope the turtles were freed at high tide. No one knew Miss Neap—her life, her loneliness, and her suffering. "She was just

Miss Neap" (160), William says. As just a name, she joins many named characters scattered throughout Pinter's plays whose representation is peripheral, thereby suggesting a particular kind of tangential being by which people touch and glance off one another, making experience alienating rather than shared. How many times Miss Neap might have cried, like the elderly Ellen in *Silence,* "Around me sits the night. Such a silence" (201), can only be surmised.

The fact of bed-sitter existence obviously stresses this solitariness, which is emphasized in Neaera knowing more about her pet water beetle than she does her hearty yet mysterious neighbor, Mr. Johnson. For the expression of this peripheral aspect of existence in its purest form, consider Neaera's overhearing this one poignant line from an anonymous girl with a man near the aquarium: "No. It's too late. It's too late" (117). That is all; no more is heard, and the scene changes. In William's bookshop the staff learn that "Penrose" has died. He is known to the manager and to William but not to the audience, and this is typical of Pinter's use of proper names throughout his work (fortunately, Penrose survives [see 110, 134]).[5] Pinter stresses urban life as peripheral encounter particularly in his film work, with his fondness for the Hitchcockian "signature."

Perhaps *The Servant* provides the best example, in an original scene by Pinter in a Soho restaurant (19–32). This contributes to the main story, with Tony's girlfriend, Susan, elaborating on her strong distaste for Barrett. Intercut between this conversation are snatches of speech from the surrounding tables, including a bishop and his curate (played by Pinter's old friend, the playwright Alun Owen); a "society woman" and a "society man," as the dramatis personae puts it, with Pinter playing the man; and an older and a younger woman. Each conversation provides a brief fragmentary insight into other lives, problems, and situations, and then it is over, and they are seen no more; they are quite tangential to the main plot, as indeed all lives are to others, inevitably, given the conditions of urban life. One recent acknowledgment made this very clear. Donald Pleasance, the actor who played Davies in *The Caretaker* on stage and screen has pointed out that, in the film of the play, the stocky mackintoshed figure who walks past Davies in the opening London street scene, his back to the audience, was Pinter himself—a Hitchcockian signature perhaps, but much more a paradigm for Pinter's work as a whole.[6]

Reunion (1989)

Reunion, Fred Uhlmann's novel of 1985, depicts the rise of nazism in 1930s Germany, the Germany Otto Beck returned to. In *Langrishe, Go Down* the private world of the Langrishes is portrayed, whereas in *Reunion* the blossoming relationship of the aristocrat Konradin von Lohenburg and Hans Strauss, son of a middle-class Jewish doctor, is set firmly against the public advent of fascism. The subject of the novel is close to Pinter's artistic concerns, since friendship and betrayal run through his work, and, second, in a recent interview Pinter acknowledged that his personal sense of Jewishness was "to identify with Jewish suffering" and that "the Holocaust is actually the most appalling thing that has ever happened."[7]

The film depicts the return of Hans (now Henry) from America to Germany after fifty-five years, ostensibly to face up to dealing with his parents' possessions, which have been in storage since the 1930s, but also subconsciously he is impelled to trace what happened to his only real schoolmate of all those years ago, Konradin. In the Stuttgart warehouse, amid his parents' furniture, he opens a tea chest of his own abandoned possessions and comes across a Corinthian coin, presented to him by Konradin at the height of their friendship, anticipating the revelation of Henry's ulterior motive.

Within the cinematic frame of Henry's quest the friendship of the two boys is recalled. Both share a collector's interest in antiquities. Hans offers his knowledge of German, French, Russian, and English literature to the eager Konradin, who, as the son of an ambassador, shares his worldly experience of different countries—all against the mixed backdrop of the beauty of the Black Forest, explored on a cycling holiday, and the ugliness of anti-Semitism encroaching like a blight on nature. Hans's classroom appraisal of *Hamlet* is scorned for his reference to Sigmund Freud as a Jew. Increasing political activity is glimpsed all around, and then Hans's neighbor's house is burned down and their children killed. Konradin is forced to reveal that his mother is rabidly anti-Semitic. A fascist history teacher condones racist bullying. An inflammatory poster is displayed by a Nazi outside the Strauss home, whereupon the doctor appears in his World War I officer's uniform and sword, decorated with an Iron Cross First Class. Arguing with a Zionist supporter, Dr. Strauss declares, "This is the land of Goethe, of Schiller, of Beethoven" (69). Proud German and proud Jew, he refuses to see the rise of Hitler as anything more than a "temporary illness."

SCREENPLAYS, 1971–93

With the Nazi accession to power even Konradin is eventually won over from his former contempt, while the Strausses pack off Hans to an American uncle. Cultured, assimilationist, irremovably German and Jewish, the Strausses symbolically anticipate the fate of a whole people by committing suicide—with gas. Henry finally discovers a memorial plaque to his school contemporaries, from which he learns of the death of his anti-Semitic tormentors in the war and finds that Konradin was executed for complicity in the 1944 attempted coup against Hitler. A somber and pitiful sense of waste prevails, but there is a degree of mitigation in Konradin's act. His sacrifice not only atones for the betrayal of friendship but symbolically atones for the larger self-betrayal of Germany. Hans and Konradin's early trust is vindicated, and the darkness of fascism could not extinguish truth for all Germans.

Within the frame of Henry's visit and discovery Pinter develops the technique he explored throughout *The Proust Screenplay* and in the opening of *Victory:* proleptic serial montage. Various images—the 1944 execution room and prison yard, the Strauss's neighbors in their garden, Konradin entering the classroom for the first time—are superimposed on Henry sitting in Central Park in 1987. Intermittently, flashes of personal memory or public images of moment are used to supplement the narrative, endowing the image with greater significance than that of mere object or event. This technique complements the scene in the Stuttgart warehouse, in which Henry confronts the fragments of memory and history, a Germany he shut from his mind fifty-five years ago. The painful mosaic of the past is reassembled as the film progresses, the sporadic ravings of the Fascist Judge Friesler finally falling into place as he raves against the anti-

Hitler conspirators, among whom, it is finally revealed, is Konradin.

The Heat of the Day (1989)

The central affair of Elizabeth Bowen's novel (1948) is between Stella, an upper-class divorcée, and Robert, an officer wounded in Dunkirk, who is now working for the War Office. Harrison, a British counterintelligence agent, has evidence of Robert's passing secrets to the enemy, and, while carrying out surveillance, he has conceived a powerful desire for Stella. In due course she tells Robert, who eventually admits his espionage, after returning to see her rather than trying to escape. Then, evading his pursuers, Robert is killed by falling, or being pushed, from the rooftop of Stella's flat.

Pinter's screenplay is extraordinarily faithful to the novel's varying forms of betrayal, and much of the seemingly Pinteresque dialogue is from Elizabeth Bowen. The major shift in the screenplay is the depiction of Harrison's passion. In the novel Harrison's desire is uncomplicated by romantic feelings. In the film, from the outset, a different perspective is provided. The opening shots before the credits find Harrison, his back to the audience, examining his surveillance photographs of Robert and Stella. Initially, foreboding music lightens to a social ambience, and then, as Harrison selects a photograph of Stella alone reclining in a park deck chair and pins it to the wall, a marked romantic motif declares itself in the music, and the camera shifts lovingly to the photograph. Her reclining posture recurs in the film. Photographs are literal and symbolic in the screenplay, both part of Harrison's work and icons of his obsession. Pinter supplied a romantic motive for Bowen's antiromantic pragmatist: "The first time I saw you . . . you were lying quite like this . . . on the grass in Regent's Park. Your eyes were closed. Then you opened your eyes and you looked up at the sky. You didn't know I was watching every move you made. . . . And then it got worse. . . . And now it's hell" (46).

The purely romantic strain in the dialogue is partly subverted by the visual representation. In each of these instances of Stella fulfilling her iconic role for Harrison, what Bowen calls her "sculpted erectness" becomes in the film more angularly cranial. The lighting and camera undermine the palimpsest of beauty in her features, revealing a faintly rebarbative hardness. Similarly, Harrison's guarded, witness box ductility is surrendered as his eyelids and jowls seem to sag in cumbersome worship. Harrison appears to separate the means, blackmail, from the ends of his kind of love, consummation. Presumably, this is the necessary morality of espionage. Yet not once does he touch Stella. Given the repeated icon of Stella, for Harrison to make love would amount to iconoclasm. Proud to be her "escort," he seems to glimpse this insight on rejecting her with a sudden access of disguised emotion, when at last desire becomes a form of understanding, however inchoate. How much, in both Bowen and Pinter, isn't known. "It wasn't going to work out" (102), Harrison recalls at the close of the film. The ideal of love is neither redeemed nor debased; it is merely human. Yet with Robert the case is different.

Harrison betrays the country by betraying his duty, and he almost allows desire to betray love. Robert betrays his country as a committed Fascist. "I was born wounded. My father's son"

(93), he says. Fascism reidentifies his future and saves him from the past and his father. Robert also betrays love, the assumed mutuality of love's knowledge in openness, which comes with posterotic fulfillment, the obverse of Harrison's arrested emotional stumbling. Yet Harrison had perceptively remarked that, "if a man were able to act being in love, he'd be enough of an actor to get away with anything" (22). This is ironically echoed by Robert later when he reproaches Stella for not immediately confronting him with Harrison's knowledge: "How well you've acted with me for the last two months" (66). His proposal of marriage seems further calculated to subvert the romantic—a wife can't testify against her husband. In spite of antipathy for Robert's confession of political faith, Stella's love responses confirm his flight to her as a sacrifice for love: "I was in terror of never seeing you again. I knew I was in danger" (95); "I had to hold you in my arms once more" (98). Parodically, from the outset Harrison knows he could be "sunk" for his conduct. The sense of mock romantic by means of likeness and contrast is brought out most tellingly at the close, when Harrison reveals his first name, Robert, and in the novel Stella reveals that she is to marry an unnamed cousin. In the film compact wins over contingency, and, in the midst of bomb sites, love's embers smoulder, albeit acridly, in this not-so-brief encounter.

The Comfort of Strangers (1990)

Photographs, obsession, and fascism arise again in Pinter's screenplay of 1990 from Ian McEwan's novel of 1981, but in a considerably more disturbing way. As the camera pans across a

Venetian apartment at the opening of the screenplay, it draws attention to "*a Nikon camera with a zoom lens and strips of developed film, on a shelf*" and to a further group of male accessories conspicuously dating from earlier this century. The objects' significance, including "*several cut-throat razors arranged in a fan*" (3), remains temporarily unexplained, but the audience is reminded repeatedly of the camera by an unseen person surreptitiously photographing Colin on holiday in Venice with his partner, Mary, both hoping to reorientate their relationship—to some degree successfully, as they rediscover intense passion. Intermittently, a white-suited, yet sinister figure, bearing a camera, shadows them, until late one night he introduces himself as Robert and guides the tourists to his bar. The objects in the apartment are the collected accessories of Robert's father and grandfather, a memorial like his repeated mention of cemetery island, their burial place.

At one stage in the film Mary notices a single photograph of Colin in Robert's apartment. Only toward the close does Caroline, Robert's wife, reveal to her a whole wall of their bedroom covered with photographs of Colin for them to gaze on while making love. Pinter saw the means of contributing to the coherence of the visual structure of the film, by implicating the enigmatic Robert and camera immediately. Unfortunately, the director, Paul Schrader, in the shooting script removed some of the photography references, made the opening pan far too general, thereby losing Pinter's emphasis on the objects, and replaced Pinter's original inclusion of an aria sung by Beniamino Gigli at the outset and intermittently throughout with heavily foreboding music by Angelo Badalamenti.

Against the romance of Venice the sentimental operatic aria

is played by Robert in his apartment at the outset. In contrast to the romantic aria, Robert is a bisexual sadist. Gigli's career spanned Robert's father and grandfather's era, the period of Mussolini and fascism. In listening to Gigli, Robert is partly re-enacting and recreating the unacknowledged trauma of his childhood. In his mesmeric voice-over narrative—begun partially at the outset, then extended with compulsive completion before Colin and Mary, and finally begun again before the chief inspector at the close—Robert reveals his intense love-hatred for his tyrannical and sadistic father. Robert "revered" and "feared" his father (10). "He was a God" (17), he explains. By adding these patterning speeches to the film, Pinter provided a more emphatic structure than the novel.

The homosexual aspect of Robert's bisexuality was lessened in the final shooting script. Initially, Robert is dressed in black, as are all the other men in his bar, with its distinct macho-homosexual ambience, and in the novel it is Robert who kisses Colin before killing him, not Caroline. Robert's philosophy of machismo fascism is the obverse of a sadomasochistic relationship, during which, at one point, in orgasmic violence, he broke his wife's back. Robert holds women in contempt and glorifies the male: "Now women treat men like children, because they can't take them seriously. But men like my father and my grandfather women took very seriously. There was no uncertainty, no confusion" (29).

In the dark undertow of sex beneath the cultured facade of Venice, the insatiable logic of perversion leads to the slaughter of Colin and copulation in his blood—a horror definitely indicated in the screenplay but modified in production. Yet Robert's perversity has considerable complexity. At one point he decries homosexuality; at another he pretends to fellow Venetians that Colin is his lover. In the screenplay, initially, he wears a gold chain with "*a gold imitation razor blade*" (13). Later he points out a barber shop formerly patronized by his father and grandfather. The father would never allow anyone in the household to get up until he had finished shaving in the bathroom. This symbolic coherence is innocently emphasized with Colin cutting himself while shaving. Finally, Robert uses one of those cutthroat razors picked out by the camera pan at the outset to slit Colin's throat. Yet, in spite of plans to leave immediately for Canada, "You leave your razor with your own fingerprints" (50), the puzzled detective tells Robert. Love and hatred are so intermixed in Robert's contorted psyche that it is impossible to know how far he is metaphorically killing his father and himself as well as Colin, who is sacrificed as the "God" (46) he has become for Robert and Caroline.

Pinter is renowned in his screenplays for his accuracy and faithfulness to the texts he works on. In *The Comfort of Strangers,* however, with Ian McEwan's approval, he inserted dialogue not found in the novel. At one stage, in the dinner scene at Robert's apartment, Mary queries "freedom" in contemporary Britain, drawing from her host a brief panegyric: "The English government is going in the right direction. In Italy we could learn a lot of lessons from the English government" (30–31). Between the publication date of McEwan's novel and the film production, the United Kingdom had undergone a number of political changes that were to affect radically Pinter's view of politics and play writing in the 1980s.

The Trial (1993)

Kafka, along with Beckett, was the most influential writer in Pinter's early reading: "When I read them it rang a bell, that's all, within me. I thought—something's going on here which is going on in me too."[8] The style of Pinter's treatment of Kafka's text was anticipated in an interview of the 1960s in commenting upon Alain Resnais's surrealistic direction of *Last Year in Marienbad* (1961), from the novel by Alain Robbe-Grillet: "The very ordinariness of the surroundings and apparent normality of the characters" in an everyday Paris café scene would be "more interesting to explore."[9]

Substitute Orson Welles's *The Trial* of 1962 for *Marienbad,* and the statement becomes the basis for Pinter's Kafka. Welles was deeply influenced by the expressionist cinema of the 1930s, which showed in *Citizen Kane* (1941), and he made that the controlling style for *The Trial.* While Kafka wrote in a period when the expressionist theater was evolving, his own style is that of a plain storyteller of a conventional, unsophisticated, simple mode, as the first words of his novel, used as epigraph by David Jones, make plain: "Someone must have been telling lies about Josef K, for without having done anything wrong he was arrested one fine morning."

Pinter has always disliked abstraction of any sort, particularly in allegorical criticism of his plays, believing that his work should be presented in a concrete, realistic fashion. This is resoundingly the case with his version of *The Trial.* In fact, it is even more concrete than Kafka, since "what is not in the script is Kafka's analysis, or K's interior monologue": "Actually I believe that it *is* there, except that it's not expressed in the same way. It's not a novel, it's a film. The thing to do was simply to show what happens, rather than discuss it."[10]

The film was made on location in Prague, and thus the story is historically and socially placed in the Austro-Hungarian Empire shortly before World War I. The opening sets the tone: Prague in early morning with shops opening up, people going about their everyday business, dusting and cleaning. In costume design and color photography everything has been done to avoid the pristine "feel" of "costume drama." Everything looks lived in and customary—hats, clothes, vehicles, streets, rooms—and is consistently followed through, even when moving to studio work elsewhere in Prague. As the film begins, Carl Davis's musical composition features an accordion—nothing could be less menacing. Thereafter, this is complemented by a slow mid-European concert waltz with a deliberate gaucheness, as if mimicking a dancer heavily out of step. It is Josef K, the senior bank clerk, who awakes to find that things are no longer in step.

On the morning of his thirtieth birthday Josef K is arrested, but he is allowed to continue working, since no charge is specified. K is contemptuous of the first court hearing to which he has been summoned and rejects its procedure. K's uncle seeks help from the lawyer Huld, a senior figure who moves in influential circles. Further advice is sought from Titorelli, the painter of court judges. Everywhere he turns, K finds legions of silent, accused men fearfully awaiting judgment, yet no one seems able to give him any concrete information about his supposed crime. Process and procedure are everything. In German the title of Kafka's parable is *Der Prozess,* which provides a richly suggestive range of metaphor: process, lawsuit, proceedings, a judgment (on one's case). Self-sustaining bureaucratic hierarchy, each level insisting on its own process and privilege, is Kafka's legalistic target of the contemporary world, with the individual caught forever in its documentary, mechanistic workings. But this is only one dimension of a story whose very simplicity leaves it open to continual interpretation. In the cathedral K confronts a priest, who expounds for him the workings of the Law in the fable of the man who seeks admission by way of a doorkeeper, who finally closes the door on the man seemingly without realizing his own futility before an ineffable God. Both are caught in a process without judgment.

The screenplay from Kafka is extremely faithful, but Pinter allows himself a signature in a slight addition at one point. Seeking the venue for his first hearing, K pretends to be looking for Lanz, a plumber, in order to take the opportunity of gaining access into different parts of the building. In Kafka he finally stumbles on a washerwoman, who admits him to the hearing. In Pinter's screenplay a little encounter is inserted:

> SECOND STAIRMAN: Ah. Lanz, yes. Yes, yes there used to be a
> man called Lanz on the fifth floor. That's right. I
> remember. He was a plumber. Definitely. But I haven't
> been up there for years.
> JOSEF K: On the fifth floor?
> SECOND STAIRMAN: I've got no reason to go up there now, you see.
> JOSEF K: Thank you.

> (18)

The mature Pinter, after a lifetime's writing, working on a text from his youth, decided on a small tribute by inserting lines

reminiscent of Mr. Kidd in his first play, *The Room,* and provided a Herr Lanz, who may or may not be real. Like Stanley in
The Birthday Party, K is led off, but to a quarry by two bizarre
figures, who, according to their own little ritual, execute him
with a knife through the heart. Just before his death a figure in
an upper story far above, overlooking the quarry, opens the windows wide and leans out, arms outspread. K responds, with raised
arms, as he dies.

At each stage K encounters females to whom he is sexually
attracted. From an old-fashioned point of view of the work as a
morality play, it is suggested that K refuses to face his meta-
physical fate by turning to sensuality. The figure in the window
may be symbolic of God, as the gesture implies, or just someone
taking the air. Alternatively, K's moral resistance makes him an
existential hero, who finally dies objecting, as his last words
indicate, "like a dog!" (66). In Harold Pinter's view: "One of the
captions that I would put on *The Trial* is simply: 'What kind of
game is God playing?' That's what Josef K is really asking. And
the only answer he gets is a pretty brutal one."[11] In a recently
published poem entitled "God" it is as if Pinter had been medi-
tating further on Kafka and Josef K, for God "had no blessing to
bestow."[12]

Notes

1. *The Proust Screenplay,* viii.
2. *Ibid.,* vii.
3. "*Victory:* A Pinter Screenplay Based on the Conrad Novel,"
The Pinter Review (1991): 23–32.

4. *Victory* (London: Methuen, 1915), 379.

5. See Ronald Knowles, "Names and Naming in the Plays of Harold Pinter," in *Harold Pinter: You Never Heard Such Silence,* edited by Alan Bold (London and Totowa, N.J.: Vision Press, Barnes and Noble, 1985).

6. In an interview before a BBC showing of the film, 1993.

7. "The 22 from Hackney to Chelsea," 15.

8. "The Rising Generation—A Playwright—Harold Pinter," interview with John Sherwood, 3 March 1960, BBC transcript, 7.

9. John Russell Taylor, "Accident," *Sight and Sound* 25, no. 4 (1966): 183–84.

10. *The Trial, Production Notes.* Courtesy of Harold Pinter.

11. *Ibid.*

12. *The Times Literary Supplement,* 24 December 1993, 21.

CHAPTER EIGHT

Plays, 1984–93:
One for the Road, Mountain Language, Party Time, Moonlight

The Political Plays—Overview

The context for the political plays—*One for the Road, Mountain Language,* and *Party Time*—is the world of public events in the 1980s, in both national and international terms. Events in the United Kingdom, the United States, South America, Turkey, and elsewhere, forced upon Pinter an urgent awareness of the imperative need for public commitment both in life and art. This chapter will survey Pinter's public engagement, with particular stress on his own statements in the period, as background to the passionate indignation that gives rise to the plays.[1]

Political awakening was not a sudden conversion. As a young man, Pinter refused to do his national service after the war on political, not moral, grounds. His refusal was not as a pacifist but because of the postwar political situation: "I disapproved of the Cold War and wasn't going to join the Army in order to help it along as a boy of 18."[2] If he had been older, he would have fought in the war. In the 1970s Pinter became a member of the Campaign for Nuclear Disarmament, and for many years he has been a member of PEN International, the organization concerned with the rights and welfare of writers throughout the world, a supporter of Amnesty International, and a subscriber to the Index on Censorship. An action that anticipated Pinter's public commitment was his attempt to deliver a letter of protest concerning the imprisonment of the Russian dissident Vladimir Bukovsky to the Russian ambassador in London and then his outlining of his concern in a letter to the *Times* (22 March 1974, 17). In relation to Pinter's later political reassessment of *The Hothouse* as reflecting the political abuse of a totalitarian society, Bukovsky's "crime" was "for criticizing the Soviet Government's use of psychiatric hospitals for political prisoners." The "Letter to Peter Wood" concerning the first production of *The Birthday Party* was published in 1981,[3] anticipating the full political revision of Pinter's views in recent interviews.

Looking back on the early plays, Pinter saw them as "metaphors" for political situations,[4] but in a television interview with John Tusa, a leading political journalist, Pinter was more explicit: "Well, they seemed to do . . . all of them seemed to do with various kinds of abuses. First of all descriptions of authoritarian systems of one kind or another, authoritarian structures. *The Hothouse* went even further and could be defined as a totalitarian society. In other words, each of the plays, I would say, dealt with the individual at the mercy of a certain authoritarian system."[5] Further comment in another television interview clarifies this: "When you look at them, they're much closer to an extremely critical look at authoritarian postures—state power, family power, religious power, power used to undermine, if not destroy the individual, or the questioning voice, or the voice which simply went away from the mainstream and refused to become part of an easily recognizable set of standards and social values."[6] It was in the Tusa interview that Pinter stated more explicitly than anywhere else the catalyst for his changed political attitudes: "The military coup in 1973 in Chile which overthrew a democratically elected government was brought about, I believe, by the United States of America . . . [this] told me without any further ado that I could not sit back and not take responsibility for my own actions, my own thoughts and act upon them which I've been doing ever since, making a bit of a nuisance of myself, in fact."

The conscientious self-examination contrasts markedly with earlier attitudes—"I came to view politicians and political structures and political acts with something I can best describe as detached contempt."[7] The reverse of this patrician aloofness eventually impelled Pinter to a point of self-recriminating candor. A TV news item covering a show at the Barbican London, on behalf of imprisoned writers, briefly interviewed Pinter, who was performing, and recorded this statement:

> I in common with a great body of people have been sleep-walking for many years, really, and I remember years ago I regarded myself as an artist in an ivory tower—really when it comes down to it a rather classic nineteenth century idea. I've now totally rejected that and I find that the things that are actually happening are not only of the greatest importance but [have] the most crucial bearing on our lives, including this matter of censorship of people and writers' imprisonment, torture, and the

whole question of how we are dealt with by governments who are in power . . . and essentially to do with the nuclear situation.[8]

The facts of torture were really brought home when Pinter joined Arthur Miller for a week-long visit to Turkey, sponsored by PEN, where he confronted the full horror of systematic torture of prisoners held for forty-five days incommunicado. Amnesty International eventually included Pinter and Miller's findings in a report, which the press summarized with the statement: "More than a quarter of a million people have been arrested on political grounds in Turkey since the 1980 military coup, and almost all have been tortured."[9] Pinter subsequently became president of the Friends of Turkey in the United Kingdom, protesting in a letter to the *Guardian* the torture, during their five-year custody, of trade unionists for engaging in basic trade union activities. More immediately germane to *Mountain Language* was Pinter's discovery of the plight of the Kurds in Turkey: "They're not really allowed to exist at all and certainly not allowed to speak their own language."[10]

In his protest at the abuse of human rights in the 1980s Pinter was frequently impelled to defend Nicaragua against the activities of the United States administration. At the end of 1987 Pinter launched an Arts for Nicaragua Fund at the Royal Court Theatre, having published the previous day a full statement of his criticism of the United States' support for the Contras: "The US Elephant must be stopped."[11] Pinter draws immediate attention to the judgment of the International Court of Justice at The Hague, in June 1986, which found that, in Pinter's words: "The US, by training, arming, equipping, financing and supplying the Contra force or otherwise encouraging, supporting and aiding military activities in and against Nicaragua, had breached its obligations under international law not to intervene in the affairs of another state." Pinter points out that the Nicaraguan revolution overthrew "a dictatorship which had been supported by the US for 40 years." The 1984 free elections were witnessed by seventy-nine observers from all over the world. Moreover, Amnesty International found that in the new Nicaragua, the systematic torture carried out in the majority of South American countries did not take place. Far from the Sandinistas being "Marxist-Leninist anti-religious devils," Nicaragua is a Catholic country with three priests as government ministers, and, while hundreds of priests had been killed in Central America in the last ten years, not one had died in Nicaragua. Pinter indicts the United States for bringing down the legally elected democracies of Guatemala in 1954 and of Chile in 1973, and the article closes with his fears for the country in which the United States–backed Contras, compared by President Reagan to the Founding Fathers, "have murdered and mutilated. . . . Thousands of Nicaraguan men, women and children"—"They have been raped, skinned, beheaded, castrated."

All this could be construed as simply anti-American propaganda were the facts not so blatant, but behind Pinter's stance there is something broader, something that was just touched on at the end of the 1984 TV news item. Apart from a piece on El Salvador, the Barbican program on imprisoned writers focused on Eastern Europe. The final exchange was as follows:

> PINTER: The horrors which are going on in Central America actually at this very [moment] . . . there's nothing to choose between one side or the other really.

INTERVIEWER: You're not lined up politically to East or West,
    Left or Right?
PINTER: Not at all.
INTERVIEWER: It's totalitarianism?
PINTER: And hypocrisy . . . which is to do with both Russia,
    America and this country.

In the Tusa interview Pinter discussed an impulse behind *One for the Road*. Both in Turkey and throughout the world there were those who would not face the reality of torture, those who "were looking at a table which had a very strong table cloth on it and vases of flowers on it": "It looked strong, that's right, and beautiful, worth preserving. They didn't look under the table at any time. Under the table they would have found what the people who are being tortured find. Mess, pain, humiliation, vomit, excrement, blood." In the same interview, as an example of "the distinctions between one reality and another," Pinter quoted the U.S. physicist Peter Hagelstein, who saw nuclear weapons as "an interesting physics problem." To Pinter the "reality" of the U.S. submarine force's nuclear capacity of destroying twenty-three thousand Hiroshimas is "death but more and more and more and more": "Other people see it in terms of strategic principles and so on. I see it in terms of annihilation." Statistics, logistics, and theoretical strategy, to Pinter, are abstract misrepresentations of the unequivocal facts of suffering and death. A graphic illustration of this was his reply to the U.S. ambassador in Turkey, who remarked that there were many opinions on any given issue: "Not if you've got an electric wire hooked to your genitals."[12] In political terms, for Pinter: "There's only one reality, you know. You can interpret reality in various ways. But there's only one. And if that reality is thousands of people being tortured to death at this very moment and hundreds of thousands of megatons of nuclear bombs standing there waiting to go off at this very moment, then that's it. . . . It has to be faced."[13]

Another kind of pressing reality that had to be faced was that of the United Kingdom itself under the ten-year rule of Thatcherism, which Pinter saw as "becoming very, very close to any other damn police state."[14] For all the significance of the visit to Turkey as "background" for *Mountain Language,* Pinter remarked: "In fact the play isn't about Turkey at all. I think the play is very much closer to home and I believe it reflects a great deal that is happening in this country."[15] He continues by indicating areas in which "the present government is turning a stronger and stronger vice on democratic institutions that we've taken for granted for a very long time"[16]—namely, Clause 28 (making "promotion" of homosexuality illegal), the Official Secrets Act, police powers, antiunion legislation, the independence of the universities, broadcasting, and the press.

Given all this, a growing sense of public dismay, frustration, and anger culminated in Charter 88, to which, along with some six thousand others, Pinter added his signature. It is ironic that the values Pinter would most support, as Charter 88 indicates, are those of the Constitution of the United States, which derive, like those of the playwright's fierce moral stance, from the values of the Enlightenment—freedom from any form of oppression, liberty of conscience, and equality before the law— in a word, democracy. This is the all-informing principle against which the plays of this period should be seen.

One for the Road (1984)

Pinter was recently dubbed a "Foucauldian *avant la lettre,*"[17] and it is not difficult to see why. The French sociologist and philosopher Michel Foucault, from the 1970s on, was particularly concerned with power in society, particularly the way in which various discourses operate both on and within individuals as a form of defining coercion. From an English point of view the seventeenth-century political philosopher Thomas Hobbes had anticipated Foucault in his conviction that, for all the appearances of man in society, the reality beneath was that of egoistic striving for power. Pinter's writings have always shown a consistent concern with direct and indirect forms of power—physical, social, and oral—and their criticism has always recognized the topic of power-subservience relationships.

One for the Road is a study not so much of torture as of the torturer, and, though ostensibly the play is concerned with the power of the torturer over the tortured, it is more subtle than that. The pathological power to corrupt the mind is made manifest, and the torturer himself is always the first victim.

In a sparse formal office that could be anywhere Nicolas interviews, in succession, a father, son, and mother—Victor, Nicky, and Gila—and then the father once more. Characters names have been chosen for their indeterminacy, and no particular country is ever mentioned. No physical violence takes place onstage. Both Victor and Gila have been beaten offstage and the latter raped several times. We do not learn of Victor's supposed offense beyond the fact that he seems to be out of step with "the man who runs this country" and his regime. "We are all patriots, we are as one, we all share a common heritage. Except you, apparently" (373), Nicolas alleges.

The victims say very little; the power of the play has to derive from the actors' ability to create a palpable sense of fear and terror. This was so much the case with Alan Bates's performance as Nicolas in the first production that the actress playing Gila, Jenny Quayle, almost underwent a nervous breakdown. Yet a corrosive, sardonic humor comes from the sick mind of Nicolas. For Pinter the politics of the 1980s were "past a joke."[18] The action takes place after the victims' torture and interrogation, demonstrating Nicolas's particular sort of sadism, which is not to actually give physical pain but, instead, to relish the broken figures before him, as his interrogation serves no practical purpose at all. "One for the Road" is Nicolas's toast as he drinks constantly throughout the interview, and this action becomes a shocking manifestation of the self-willed intoxication of power: "I love death," he says. "The death of others. Do you love the death of others, or at any rate do you love the death of others as much as I do? . . . Death. Death. Death. Death. As has been noted by the most respected authorities, it is beautiful. The purest, most harmonious thing there is" (370–71). Absolute for death, with the power to take or give life, Nicolas even goes in for a little fascist pleasantry: "Everyone else knows the voice of God speaks through me" (368).

Invoking civilization and civility, friendship and respect, the corruption of his mind is in the corruption of his language, as he also talks of "wet shit," of his agents, who "pissed on the rugs" (369). Nicolas's strategy becomes apparent in Victor's eventual comment, "Kill me" (373). To reduce life to a condition worse than death and then to refrain from actual killing is the last refinement of the sadist.

Gila is simply bludgeoned verbally by Nicolas's hatred until she inadvertently mentions her father, which draws a revealing outburst from Nicolas, who celebrates the father's patriotism, his heroism, and his faith: "He would die, he would die, he would die for his country, for his God. . . . How dare you speak of your father to me? I loved him, as if he were my own father" (381). It is a fascism like that of Robert's in *The Comfort of Strangers* in the association of death, the death wish, and God with the loved/hated father figure. When he interviews Nicky, Nicolas is fatherly and talks of airplanes and toys. As in the interpretation of the father figure in *The Birthday Party,* so here the father figure sacrifices his namesake. Answering Victor's pained inquiry, Nicolas's closing line is: "Your son? Oh, don't worry about him. He was a little prick" (387).

Mountain Language (1988) and "New World Order" (1991)

Mountain Language concerns a group of women who have been waiting all day outside a prison in the hope of seeing their menfolk inside. They have to endure abuse from an intimidating sergeant, and in one case an elderly woman has almost had a thumb severed by a guard dog. On admission to the prisoners "mountain language" is forbidden, and prisoners and visitors must use the language of the capital. It was assumed that Pinter had written a barely veiled critique of Turkey's suppression of the Kurds and their language, but he resisted the identification, suggesting that the play has a certain significance for an English audience. Pinter's very short work of less than a thousand words can be seen in both a literal and metaphorical way.

From a literal point of view an audience is likely to make the connection with the plight of the Kurds, though Brian Friel's play of 1980, *Translations,* reminded a British audience of the English encroachment on the Irish language in the nineteenth century. Friel's play was well attended in Wales, where it is not forgotten that England attempted to prohibit the speaking of Welsh in the last century. Throughout the performance of *Mountain Language* Pinter, as director, created a particular uneasiness in the audience by exploiting a specific condition of audience reception. The soldiers are dressed in regular battle fatigues, and the foul-mouthed sergeant spoke with a strong London accent. British television screens have made British audiences long familiar with such images—in the Northern Ireland of the "H" blocks, no-go areas, proscription on broadcasting interviews with representatives of the IRA. By having political and geographical reference undetermined, but suggested, Pinter creates a polemical space in which the question arises just how far the United Kingdom could be said to have taken such a direction.

Pinter signals this in a fashion that is peculiarly his own. No British dramatist has used names and naming so consistently throughout a whole career as Pinter has.[19] Let one example stand for many. In *Betrayal* the only time that the married name and titles of Robert and Emma are mentioned is precisely when Robert comes across Jerry's letter to Emma in the American Express office in Venice and intuitively realizes the nature of the contents: "I mean, just because my name is Downs and your name is Downs doesn't mean that we're the Mr. and Mrs. Downs that they, in their laughing Mediterranean way, assume we are" (218). Approximately halfway through *Mountain Language* one of the women reveals that her name is the very English "Sara Johnson." In contrast to the names in *One for the Road,* this comes as a shock if it is automatically assumed that such abuses could only happen in places like Turkey.

The first word of *Mountain Language* is "Name?" and this aspect of bureaucratic officialdom is cruelly parodied when one of the women complains of the older woman's injury from the dog. The officer in charge insists that he can only initiate disciplinary procedures if he is given the name of the animal: "Every dog has a *name!* They answer to their name. They are given a name by their parents and that is their name, that is their *name.* Before they bite they *state* their name. It's a formal procedure" (393). Beyond this overt bullying there is a certain kind of profundity.

The old woman is forbidden to speak her mountain language, and, unlike her prisoner son, she does not speak the language of the capital. Then the decision is reversed, and mountain language is allowed. But now the old woman is traumatized by the sight of blood on her son's face and her own pain and is speechless. At this the son is reduced to a voiceless shuddering. The logic of totalitarianism always seeks to suppress speech—by book-burning, torture, murder, or exile—because speech is itself symbolic of freedom. To speak is to name things like truth and tyranny, to speak is to give one's voice in a vote, in antiquity, or to mark a ballot paper in modern democracies. The final tableau of mother and son indicates the end of democracy—the body politic made speechless. Thankfully, after sound mountains echo; that is their "language."

The sketch "New World Order" appeared as a curtain raiser for Ariel Dorfman's acclaimed play *Death and the Maiden.* Set in post-Pinochet Chile, Dorfman's work concerns a woman's revenge against her past torturer. In Pinter's sketch two interrogators gloat over their blindfolded victim, swapping obscenities, until the almost sexual sadistic climax with one sobbing and the other congratulating him for "keeping the world clean for democracy" (3). These words were those used by the youthful Pinter and friends in ironic response to the dropping of atom bombs on Japan.[20] As in *Mountain Language,* the victim is rendered literally and symbolically speechless: "Before he came in here he was a big shot, he never stopped shooting his mouth off, he never stopped questioning received ideas. Now—because he's apprehensive about what's about to happen to him—he's stopped all that, he's got nothing more to say" (2). Similarly, upon Victor's second entrance in *One for the Road* he has difficulty speaking because his torturers have mutilated his tongue.

Party Time (1991)

Another figure who wishes "to clean up . . . wash the place clean," is the Commander in the biblical dystopia of *A Handmaid's Tale,* a film from Margaret Atwood's novel. Pinter's name was kept in the credits, but he decided not to publish the screenplay, which differed in several places from the final shooting script. The handmaids are fertile young women coerced into becoming the bearers of children for a ruling elite, whose wives are sterile. The puritanical totalitarian state rejects any dissidence, and in the background of a particular handmaid's story the military regime is carrying out a violent purge against a rebellion. Atwood's slightly futuristic setting nevertheless recalls actualities of history. In 1976 Joseph Losey made *Mr. Klein,* the backdrop of which was the Vichy government's roundup of Jews in 1942. History and film provide a context for Pinter's most recent play, *Party Time,* along with the reality of increasingly autocratic government of the United Kingdom in the 1980s.

Party Time is like the obverse of the public world of these films. In Gavin's flat a party gets under way, with just a few remarks intimating that something is taking place outside. Dusty, a guest, twice tries to raise the question of her brother's whereabouts, but "it's not on anyone's agenda" (18), she is told. Dame Melissa, arriving at the party, is rather bewildered by "soldiers": "My driver had to stop at a . . . you know . . . what do you call it? . . . a roadblock. We had to say who we were . . . it really was a trifle . . ." (7). It is the measure of the distance from reality of such a character that she has to search for the word *roadblock.* Her reality is the reality of a trifling delay on the way to a party. What the reality of a roadblock is for those presumably under curfew can be imagined.

In due course, after a symbolic exchange of clenched fists and a simultaneous declaration—"A bit of that"—Fred asks: "How's it going tonight?" "Like clockwork" (13), Douglas replies. In a slightly expanded version of the play for television, additional characters, Sam, Smith, and Harlow, discuss a musician called Stoddart: "I met a man at a party the other day—I couldn't believe it—He was talking the most absolute bloody crap—his ideas about the world, that kind of thing—he was a complete and utter and total arsehole." Smith replies: "Don't worry about Stoddart. We've seen him off," and Harlow adds, in comic idiom, "We've had him for breakfast."[21] In other additional exchanges for the television production we learn that Emily's husband cannot be present, as "he's busy . . . down there" on the streets outside. What this means becomes clear when another character later lets drop that Emily's husband, the equestrian sportsman they are discussing, jumps, "for the army." All these hints culminate in Gavin, a personage of undisclosed power and influence, declaring: "Now I believe one or two of our guests encountered traffic problems an their way here tonight. I apologize for that, but I would like to assure you that all such problems and all related problems will be resolved very soon. Between ourselves, we've had a bit of a round-up this evening" (36–37). Such euphemism is chilling.

These remarks are interspersed among snatches of conversation largely revolving around the benefits of a new leisure club. Comfort, luxury, fashion, and sex alternating with a dash of fascist morality reflect the wealthy and powerful "society of beautifully dressed people," of "elegance, style, grace, taste." Yet it would be hard to find such a collection of saloon bar pieties, obscenity, crassness, and vulgarity. All are embodied in Terry, friend of the great and arbiter of "real class" (21), who recounts of his wife, Dusty: "The only thing she doesn't like on boats is being fucked on boats" (17).

Three times in the course of the play a light "*burns into the room*" through a partly opened door. Finally, Dusty's brother Jimmy enters in spectral disarray, standing in the light of the doorway. In his closing speech Pinter attempts to find language and utterance for what is left of a person after torture and deprivation, when identity, consciousness, and the senses have been pulverized and only darkness is left: "The dark is in my mouth" (38), Jimmy says.

Party Time is a punning title of great relevance for the 1980s, in which the deregulation of the money markets in England meant great wealth and one long party for the well placed few. In that decade champagne imports doubled, while it was discovered that in economically blighted areas of the country scavengers picked on rubbish heaps for a living. In reviews of the play Michael Billington, a leading critic and Pinter's forthcoming biographer, made the most incisive and just comment on the play: "a packed, swift indictment of blunted modern sensitivities . . . private relationships echo public brutality . . . an image of style-conscious, narcissistic, bourgeois society cut off from and culpably indifferent to the intolerance and squalor of the outside world."[22]

Moonlight (1993)

The genesis of *Moonlight,* the first full-length work since *Betrayal,* is more unusual than Pinter's customary engendering creative process. The play was written intensively over the Christmas holiday period of 1992–93 and the third and final draft finished at the end of January. Pinter completed the work while immersed as actor, since October 1992, in a very successful revival of his own earlier play of 1974, *No Man's Land.* Pinter played Hirst, the alcoholic writer who has retreated into the representations and misrepresentations of delusive memory. As

Pinter recorded: "When I was acting in *No Man's Land* every night, saying those words every night, and however nerve-racking an event acting is, it's also enjoyable if you get it right, I was stimulated by the act of saying these words and getting a few laughs. And one day while I was still acting at night, I started to scribble away and so something in me was released by saying all these damned words."[23]

Pinter has always maintained an absolute and objective distance from artistic creativity, as if writing involved an abnegation of self while the process takes place. Thus, he has always denied any omniscient superior knowledge of a play beyond what appears in the text itself, and characters take on a life of their own onstage—speech now theirs, no longer the author's. Paradoxically, Pinter acknowledged: "I have learned more about my own play by acting in it."[24] This position is perhaps not strange to modern audiences familiar with Pirandello's *Six Characters in Search of an Author* (1921). But, with Pinter returning to his play as an actor, there is a crucial difference from Pirandello. A group of characters are not seeking an author, but the playwright himself returns as a character and reenters his play of twenty years ago to find "pools within it that [he] hadn't known were there: as if the light hit it": "I just saw that image, I don't know why, of light hitting dark pools and illuminating those pools."[25] In returning to the 1970s—before the decade of his political involvement—with an actor's imaginative projection and immersion, Pinter found seven characters bathed in moonlight, waiting for their story to be told.

There is little action in *Moonlight*. Andy, a man in his fifties, lays in bed awaiting his death, with his wife, Bel, in attendance at his bedside. In another area of the stage two young men, Andy's estranged sons, Jake and Fred, develop endlessly prevaricating word games. Intermittently, in a third stage area there appears the wraithlike figure of a young girl, Bridget, the daughter, speaking lyrically of light and dark and the moon. On three occasions Maria and Ralph, old family friends of Andy and Bel, appear with stories of the past.

Pinter acknowledged: "Obviously as you're older you think about death more; you have it on your body; but there's so much death about," observing, "My mother died last year, she was 88." He was quick to add, "But I'm not at all sure the play comes from that fact," pointing out that he had in his possession notes from 1977: "I was writing the same thing . . . it was a man dying; a man saying, 'Where are they?'"[26] The date 1977 is significant, since that was the year his schooldays mentor and lifetime friend, Joseph Brearley his English master, died. Ten years after this death Pinter wrote a commemorative poem invoking the presence of his friend, revealingly: "You tall in moonlight." Darkness and light, moonlight and loss, separation and death, all reemerge in the creation of *Moonlight.*

David Leveaux's direction of *Moonlight* was his third of a Pinter play at the Almeida Theatre, London, following that of *Betrayal* (1991) and *No Man's Land* (1992). Common to all three productions was visual austerity—from the white of *Betrayal* to the gray of *No Man's Land* to the pallor of *Moonlight.* The small Almeida stage created a visually telling irony by necessarily having to place the beds of Andy and Fred side by side: physical closeness and yet an insurmountable emotional distance, a mode that recalls the memory plays. But then a greater irony still, whereas so many of Pinter's earliest characters had been threatened with dispossession by another person, here Andy awaits the final dispossession of all—of room, of memory, of speech, and of life itself—by the silence of death.

Although generally the play was very well received, audiences and critics had some difficulty in absorbing the play as a whole. After a long absence from the stage Ian Holm won a prestigious award for his portrayal of Andy. All critics seized on the unambiguous passion of grief and anger in Holm's flashes of rage, several quoting Dylan Thomas's "Do not go gentle into that good night / Rage, rage against the dying of the light." Pinter certainly does not provide the algebraic stepping stones of the well-made play, but on the other hand he does give what is the case with many playwrights—an evocative title. If the play is considered retroactively with this in mind, its formal coherence emerges.

In the middle of the play Bel suggests, "Death is your new horizon." Andy's reply is a major turning point in the play and is thus given extensively here:

> That may be. That may be. But the big question is, will I cross it as I die or after I'm dead? Or perhaps I won't cross it at all. Perhaps I'll just stay stuck in the middle of the horizon. In which case, can I see over it? Can I see to the other side? Or is the horizon endless? And what's the weather like? Is it uncertain with showers or sunny with fogpatches? Or unceasing moonlight with no cloud? Or pitch black for ever and ever? You may say you haven't the faintest fucking idea and you would be right. But personally I don't believe it's going to be pitch black for ever because if it's pitch black for ever what would have been the point of going through all these enervating charades in the first place? (46)

Bob Crowley, the designer, emphasized the crepuscular, throughout stressing gray, white, and black, so much so that the light fades themselves become an integral part of the play. Above all, Andy's bed/deathbed, with its silver-white covering, became a visual correlative to his state. This was taken one emphatic and revealing step further in the design for the advertising poster and the cover of the text. The poster featured the bed—empty—photographed from directly above, the canopy lit to appear silver, while on either side was blackness. A variant on this clear symbolism appeared on the book cover.

If death is a "pitch black" nothingness, as Andy ponders, then "unceasing moonlight with no cloud" precedes it as a final limbo of guilt-ridden consciousness, anticipated by the moonlit white of Andy's deathbed. This situation provides a context for the expressionist function of Bridget. She is the ghostlike projection of Andy's grief and guilt. In rehearsal, when David Leveaux asked whether Bridget was dead, Pinter replied, "That would seem to be the case."[27] Thus, as the play opens, the benign spirit of Bridget emerges in darkness: "There's no moon. It's so dark. . . . It's so dark" (1), while at the close she tells us of waiting, "I stood there in the moonlight" (80), separate from a house, which was "dark."

Bridget is the emotional core of the play. Her death is never discussed, but what she means to each of the characters through the circumstance of death—hers and Andy's—is the source of compromising pain. In contrast, the scene between Jake, Fred, and Bridget (29–33) might seem inconsequential and redundant. It is played in the "third area" of the stage, which is largely allocated to Bridget. Crucially, the printed text indicates that this is ten years ago; the boys are eighteen and seventeen, respectively, and Bridget is fourteen, just two years younger than her ghost-like appearance elsewhere in the play, since the dramatis personae gives her age as sixteen, presumably her age at death. The youthful scene simply depicts Bridget listening to music (forebodingly, Elton John's elegiac "Song for Guy" was chosen), while Fred pesters Jake to join him on a lift to a gig. Just enough is given to bring out that peculiar combination of devotion and dislike perhaps unique to siblings of both sexes. In short, the scene reminds us of the ordinariness of young people at home—all that Bridget's death destroyed. Later in the play, in the midst of mutually defensive charades, we suddenly find the following:

> FRED: Bridget would understand. I was her brother. She
>   understood me. She always understood my feelings.
> JAKE: She understood me too.
> *Pause.*
>   She understood me too.
> *Silence.*
>
> (53)

Earlier Andy, pugnaciously seeking an illicit drink, searches for a bottle in the third stage area, which now doubles as part of his house. As he drinks, the area reverts to the moonlit space for Bridget, who appears, still, in the background—of both the stage and of Andy's conscience, as he laments: "Ah darling. Ah my darling" (49). Joined by Bel in silence, they complete a mute tableau of three. Guilt, grief, and delusion have become so intermixed that Andy not only resurrects Bridget but also her unborn children. "Where is she?" Andy asks and evokes the fatherly memory of comforting her as she was falling asleep. Bel weakly remonstrates: "Please. Oh please." But after a pause Andy persists, "Is she bringing my grandchildren to see me?" as Bel "*sits frozen*" (45), while he rehearses his death and their loss. Toward the close Maria and Ralph enter, ten years after moving away, which was two years before the death of Bridget. Unknowingly, Maria recalls: "Your lovely little girl! Bridget! (*She laughs.*) Little girl! She must be a mother by now." To which Andy replies: "I've got three beautiful grandchildren (*To* BEL) Haven't I?" (71).

The "past is a mist" (20) for Andy because he cannot bring himself to confront whatever degree of responsibility, of either omission or commission, was his in Bridget's death, even at the point of his own demise. He protests, "I've never harmed a soul" (4), but his conscience belies the claim. Stories of Bel's lesbian affair with Maria in the past show that she is not beyond reproach, which is presumably the basis for Jake's "Don't talk dirty to me," when asked by Fred, "Tell me about your mother" (62). The sons' estrangement is as complete as their love must have been, since the whole of their time is spent in an obsessive parodic roll call of civil service figures—all proxies for the father they cannot name without mockery—culminating in the mock consolation for one "Silvio D'Orangerie." "I loved him like a father" (79), says Fred.

In following through these affective ramifications the serious emotional core of the play is revealed—but, of course, this is literary exposition, not the play that Harold Pinter wrote. These concerns are just part of the total experience of the play, much of which consists of hilarious foul-mouthed exchanges from Andy, as part of the fascinating collocation of the class registers of

English idiom ironically giving such vibrancy and life to the subject of death. Once again Pinter resists the conventional alliance of subject and sentiment, of death and pathos. Andy subverts the sentimental as he watches Bel embroider, querying: "Oh, I've been meaning to ask you, What are you making there? A winding sheet? Are you going to wrap me up in it when I conk out? You'd better get a move on. I'm going fast" (34).

Unsympathetic critics once again saw Pinter as repeating himself, whereas it can be said that, in the peculiar psychology that lies beneath the creation of *Moonlight,* Pinter returned to his imaginative roots and did indeed compose a work that offers something of a retrospective. Menace, as we have seen, teams up with the intruder death. The whole play could be said to be about the evasion of communication concerning Bridget. Even in death and at a distance, Andy exercises power over his sons. Memory reacts once more as the past jostles with the present. Again, the theatrical vies with realism, seriousness with laughter.

Furthermore, actual dramatic contexts are evoked constantly. The bond of isolated brotherhood, seen here between Jake and Fred, recalls that of Mick and Aston in *The Caretaker.* Andy's vulgar power in travestying the family is occasionally close to Max in *The Homecoming.* Such emotional distance between husband and wife recalls *Landscape.* The two women–one male triangle of the past, and mutual betrayal, is like a combination of *Old Times* and *Betrayal.* Andy is no Hirst, but there is something about that moonlit canopy which relates it to *No Man's Land.* Pinter's delight in rococo character and language almost throughout recalls the stylized extremes of *Family Voices.* Finally, in the bed and bedside attendant we have something of a reverse of *A*

Kind of Alaska. Yet, for all this, *Moonlight* adds to Pinter's oeuvre significantly. Nowhere else is found such expression as Andy's grief and rage—not in Hirst and not in Deeley. And *finally* is most certainly the wrong word. Pinter—vituperative, passionate, and committed—remains avidly engaged with whatever the work in hand is, be it acting, directing, writing screenplays or drama, or taking part in political activity.

Pinter changed the nature of theater experience because he intuitively grasped that the conventional representation of the individual and society on the stage was no longer a reflection of what humanity had become in the course of the twentieth century. The positivist enthronement of universal human nature, an essentialist humanism, was displaced by the less palatable truths of humanity as limited and contingent. The moral assurances of the literature of tragedy, heroism, and romance were no longer tenable for Pinter, and neither was the security of human beings in a metaphysically contained universe. In Pinter's theater humanity is stripped to the barest speech in the barest silence, against which laughter resonates uneasily.

As an individual, Harold Pinter has made a major contribution to British cultural life in the second half of the twentieth century. But he has never allowed success to soften his responses to life around him. Rigorous, challenging, and radical, his work always insists on the examination of self and society. A Socratic gadfly on the body politic—long may he remain so. A recent tribute by Pinter's contemporary, the playwright John McGrath, provides a fitting conclusion: "We ought to be glad that we've got Harold Pinter because he handles words, he believes in words and the power of words in the theater, and he has the ability to make them work."[28] Where there is comedy and there is truth, they combine to make an art that is, as Pinter once put it, "a kind of celebration."[29]

Notes

1. The factual details which follow are taken from a fuller article by the author, "Harold Pinter, Citizen," *The Pinter Review* (1989).

2. "Radical Departures," *The Listener* 120, no. 3086 (27 October 1988), 6.

3. In Michael Scott, ed., *Harold Pinter: "The Birthday Party," "The Caretaker," and "The Homecoming,"* (London: Macmillan, 1986).

4. "Radical Departures," 6, and "A Play and Its Politics. A Conversation between Harold Pinter and Nicholas Hern," preface to *One for the Road* (London: Methuen, 1984), 8.

5. "Harold Pinter Plays and Politics," BBC 2, *Saturday Review,* 28 September 1985. See Knowles, "Harold Pinter, Citizen."

6. "Radical Departures," 6.

7. "A Play and Its Politics," 12.

8. Channel Four 7 o'clock News, 9 January 1984.

9. *The Independent,* 2 November 1988, 13.

10. "Radical Departures," 4.

11. *The Guardian,* 5 December 1987, 10

12. *The Guardian,* 22 October 1988, 9.

13. "A Play and Its Politics," 21.

14. "The New Light that burns within Harold Pinter," Bryan Appleyard (an interview with Pinter), *The Times,* 16 March 1984, 13.

15. "Radical Departures," 6.

16. *Ibid.*

17. By Terry Eagleton in a review of *Party Time, Times Literary Supplement,* 15 November 1991, 20.

18. "A Play and Its Politics," 11.

19. See Knowles, "Names and Naming in the Plays of Harold Pinter," in *Harold Pinter: You Never Heard Such Silence,* edited by Alan Bold (London and Totowa, N.J.: Vision Press, Barnes and Noble, 1985).

20. "The 22 from Hackney to Chelsea," 14.

21. Typescript courtesy of Harold Pinter.

22. *The Guardian,* 7 November 1991, 32.

23. "HP Source," *Time Out,* 15–22 September 1993, 19.

24. *The Observer,* 14 February 1993, 22.

25. "Harold's New Baby," *The Guardian,* 3 February 1993, 3.

26. "HP Source," 19.

27. "Angry Old Man of the Theater," *The Observer,* 12 September 1993, 9.

28. *The Late Show,* BBC 2, 7 November 1991.

29. "Writing for the Theatre," *Plays One* (London: Faber, 1991), xiv.

CHRONOLOGY OF PINTER'S WORK

Work	Written	Performed	Published
The Room	1957	1957	1960
The Birthday Party	1957	1958	1960
The Dumb Waiter	1957	1959	1960
A Slight Ache	1958	1959	1961
The Hothouse	1958	1980	1980
The Caretaker	1959	1960	1960
Revue Sketches: "The Black and White"; "Trouble in the Works"; "Last to Go"; "Request Stop"	1959	1959	1961
"Special Offer"	1959	1959	1967
"That's Your Trouble"; "That's All"; "Interview"	1959	1964	1966
"Applicant"	1959	1964	1961
"Dialogue Three"	1959	1964	1963
A Night Out	1959	1960	1961
Night School	1960	1960	1967
The Dwarfs	1960	1960	1961

CHRONOLOGY OF PINTER'S WORK

Work	Written	Performed	Published
The Collection	1961	1961	1963
The Lover	1962	1963	1963
The Servant	1962	1963	1971
The Pumpkin Eater	1963	1964	1971
Tea Party	1964	1965	1967
The Homecoming	1964	1965	1965
The Basement	1966	1967	1967
The Quiller Memorandum	1966	1966	1971
Accident	1966	1967	1971
Landscape	1967	1968	1968
Silence	1968	1969	1969
"Night" (revue sketch)	1969	1969	1969
The Go-Between	1969	1971	1971
Old Times	1970	1971	1971
Langrishe Go Down	1971	1978	1982
The Proust Screenplay	1972	Unproduced	1978
Monologue	1972	1973	1973
No Man's Land	1974	1975	1975
The Last Tycoon	1975	1977	1982
Betrayal	1978	1978	1978
Family Voices	1980	1981	1981
The French Lieutenant's Woman	1980	1981	1981

CHRONOLOGY OF PINTER'S WORK

Work	Written	Performed	Published
A Kind of Alaska	1982	1982	1982
Victoria Station	1982	1982	1982
Victory	1982	Unproduced	1990
One for the Road	1984	1984	1984
"Precisely"	1985	1985	1985
Turtle Diary	1984	1985	1990
Mountain Language	1988	1988	1988
The Heat of the Day	1988	1989	1989
Reunion	1988	1989	1990
The Comfort of Strangers	1989	1990	1990
"New World Order"	1991	1991	1992
Party Time	1991	1991	1991
The Trial	1989	1993	1993
Moonlight	1993	1993	1993

BIBLIOGRAPHY

A Select Bibliography of Criticism in English

In recent years has appeared *The Pinter Review: Annual Essays,* published by the University of Tampa Press, Florida. Each issue contains a survey of current criticism. Steven H. Gale, *Harold Pinter: An Annotated Bibliography* (Boston: G. K. Hall, 1978), is the leading bibliography of criticism.

Books

Almansi, Guido, and Simon Henderson. *Harold Pinter*. London and New York: Methuen, 1983. A fascinating study of 'games' in Pinter.

Baker, William, and Stephen Ely Tabachnick. *Harold Pinter*. Edinburgh: Oliver and Boyd, 1973. A good chapter on Pinter's London background of the 1930s.

Burkman, Katherine H. *The Dramatic World of Harold Pinter: Its Basis in Ritual*. Columbus: University of Ohio Press, 1971. Discusses patterns of ancient fertility myth in the plays.

Byezkowska-Page, Eva. *The Structure of Time-Space in Harold Pinter's Drama, 1957–1973*. Wroclaw: University of Wroclaw Press, 1983.

Cahn, Victor L. *Gender and Power in the Plays of Harold Pinter*. Houndmills: Macmillan, 1994. A nontheoretical survey of selected plays.

Diamond, Elin. *Pinter's Comic Play*. Lewisburg, Pa: Bucknell University Press, 1985. Pursues the strained claim that Pinter's characters derive from the archetypes of comedy tradition.

BIBLIOGRAPHY

Dukore, Bernard. *Where Laughter Stops: Pinter's Tragicomedy*. Columbus and London: University of Missouri Press, 1976. An important thesis. Matters that critically give rise to laughter are finally very serious.

————. *Harold Pinter*. London and New York: Macmillan, 1982. A general survey.

Esslin, Martin. *Pinter: A Study of His Plays*. London and New York: Eyre Methuen, 1977. A third expanded edition of a work originally entitled *The Peopled Wound: The Plays of Harold Pinter* (1970). The first full-length study in English. Much biographical information and access allowed to then unpublished works of Pinter.

Gale, Steven H. *Butter's Going Up: A Critical Analysis of Harold Pinter's Work*. Durham: Duke University Press, 1977. The first study to recognize the importance of Pinter's revisions.

Gabbard, L. P. *The Dream Structure of Pinter's Plays: A Psycho-analytical Approach*. Rutherford, N.J.: Fairleigh Dickinson University Press, 1976. Predictable Freudian paradigms.

Hayman, Ronald. *Harold Pinter*. London: Heinemann, 1973. Very limited exposition.

Hinchcliffe, Arnold P. *Harold Pinter*. Boston: Twayne Publishers, 1981. A revised edition of the original Twayne publication of 1967.

Hollis, James R. *Harold Pinter: The Poetics of Silence*. Carbondale: Southern Illinois University Press, 1970.

Kerr, Walter. *Harold Pinter*. New York: Columbia University Press, 1967. A major commentator on theater with an important approach to Pinter as an existential writer. It is considerably weakened, however, by Kerr's limited understanding of existentialism.

Klein, Joanne. *Making Pictures: The Pinter Screenplays*. Columbus: Ohio State University Press, 1985.

Knowles, Ronald. *"The Birthday Party" and "The Caretaker": Text and Performance*. Houndmills and London: Macmillan, 1988. In part this study discusses leading productions of the plays.

BIBLIOGRAPHY

Korpimies, Liisa. *A Linguistic Approach to the Analysis of a Dramatic Text: A Study in Discourse Analysis and Cohesion with Special Reference to "The Birthday Party."* Jyväskylä: University of Jyväskylä Press, 1983.

Merritt, Susan Hollis. *Pinter in Play: Critical Strategies and the Plays of Harold Pinter.* Durham and London: Duke University Press, 1990. This extensive study by a leading Pinter bibliographer provides an analysis of the major critics of Pinter's work.

Quigley, Austen E. *The Pinter Problem.* Princeton: Princeton University Press, 1975. An intellectually rigorous Wittgensteinian reading.

Sakellaridou, Elizabeth. *Pinter's Female Portraits.* London and Totowa, N.J: Macmillan, 1988. A feminist reading.

Santucci, Lino Falzon. *Harold Pinter: Explorations in Verbal and Non Verbal Interaction.* Messina: Peloritana Editrice, 1981.

Schroll, Herman T. *Harold Pinter: A Study of His Reputation, 1958–1969.* Metuchen, N.J.: Scarecrow Press, 1971.

Silverstein, Marc. *Harold Pinter and the Language of Cultural Power.* Lewisburg, Pa.: Bucknell University Press, 1993. An advanced poststructuralist study of subjectivity, discourse, and ideology.

Strunk, Volker. *Harold Pinter: Towards a Poetics of His Plays.* New York: Peter Lang, 1989. Attempts an argument on Pinter as a mannerist.

Sykes, Alrene. *Harold Pinter.* Queensland and New York: Humanities Press, University of Queensland Press, 1970. Good on Pinter as a radio dramatist.

Thompson, David T. *Pinter, the Player's Playwright.* London and New York: Macmillan, 1985. A well-documented study of Pinter's career as an actor in repertory theater.

Trussler, Simon. *The Plays of Harold Pinter: An Assessment.* London: Victor Gollancz, 1973.

BIBLIOGRAPHY

Collections of Essays

Bloom, Harold, ed. *Harold Pinter: Modern Critical Views*. New York: Chelsea House Publishers, 1987.

Bold, Alan, ed. *Harold Pinter: You Never Heard Such Silence*. London and Totowa, N.J: Vision Press, Barnes and Noble, 1985.

Burkman, Katherine H., and John L. Kundert-Gibbs, eds. *Pinter at Sixty*. Bloomington and Indianapolis: Indiana University Press, 1993. Papers from the Pinter birthday festival at Ohio State University.

Gale, Steven H., ed. *Critical Essays on Harold Pinter*. Boston: G. K. Hall, 1990. A very varied collection of essays, none of which have been reprinted before.

———. *Harold Pinter. Critical Approaches*. Rutherford, N.J: Fairleigh Dickinson University Press, 1986. A collection of original essays.

Ganz, Arthur, ed. *Pinter: A Collection of Critical Essays*. Englewood Cliffs, N.J: Prentice-Hall, 1972.

Gordon, Lois, ed. *Harold Pinter: A Casebook*. New York and London: Garland Publishing, 1990. This volume includes a unique series of photos of Pinter as actor on tour in 1950s Ireland.

Lahr, John, ed. *A Casebook on Harold Pinter's "The Homecoming."* New York: Grove Press, 1971. An outstanding compilation particularly for the director, designer, and actors' discussion of rehearsal and production.

Scott, Michael, ed. *Harold Pinter, "The Birthday Party," "The Caretaker" and "The Homecoming."* London: Macmillan, 1986. A casebook, including the very important letter of Pinter to Peter Wood, the first director of *The Birthday Party*.

Selected Articles

The following is a small selection from a number of articles, details of which may be found in the annual bibliographies of the June issue of the quarterly periodical *Modern Drama;* volume 17 (December 1974) is devoted to Pinter. The bibliography section of *The Pinter Review* also includes details of "work in progress."

Armstrong, W. A. "Tradition and Innovation in the London Theatre." *Modern Drama* 4, no. 2 (1961): 184–95. Pinter and 1950s realism.

Bernhard, F. J. "Beyond Realism: The Plays of Harold Pinter." *Modern Drama* 8, no. 2 (1965): 185–91. Pinter and 1950s realism.

Cohn, Ruby. "Words Working Overtime: *Endgame* and *No Man's Land.*" *The Yearbook of English Studies* 9 (1979): 188–203.

Cook, David, and Harold F. Brooks. "A Room with Three Views: Harold Pinter's *The Caretaker.*" *Komos* 1 (1967): 62–69.

Feynman, A. C. "The Fetal Quality of 'Character' in Plays of the Absurd." *Modern Drama* 9, no. 1 (1966): 18–25.

Fuentes, Carlos. "Pinter: A Culture of Absence." *The Pinter Review* (1990): 1–3. A leading South American writer on Pinter.

Gillen, Francis. "From Chapter Ten of *The Dwarfs* to *Mountain Language:* The Continuity of Harold Pinter." *The Pinter Review* (1988): 1–7.

Hammond, B. S. "Beckett and Pinter: Towards a Grammar of the Absurd." *Journal of Beckett Studies* 4 (1979): 35–42.

Hays, H. R. "Transcending Naturalism." *Modern Drama* 5, no. 1 (1962): 27–36. The debate on realism once more.

Hughes, Alan. "'They Can't Take That Away from Me': Myth and Memory in Pinter's *Old Times.*" *Modern Drama* 17, no. 4 (1974): 467–76.

Kaufman, Michael W. "Actions that a Man Might Play: Pinter's *The Birthday Party.*" *Modern Drama* 16, no. 2 (1973): 167–78.

Knowles, Ronald. "Friendship and Betrayal in the Plays of Harold Pinter." *Long Room* nos. 28–29 (1984): 33–44.

———. "*The Hothouse* and the Epiphany of Harold Pinter." *Journal of Beckett Studies* 10 (1985): 134–44.

BIBLIOGRAPHY

———. "Names and Naming in the Plays of Harold Pinter." In *Harold Pinter: You Never Heard Such Silence.* Edited by Alan Bold, 113–30. London and Totowa, N.J.: Vision Press, Barnes and Noble, 1985.

———. "The Caretaker and the 'Point' of Laughter." Reprinted in *Harold Pinter, "The Birthday Party," "The Caretaker," and "The Homecoming."* Edited by Michael Scott, 146–61. London: Macmillan, 1986.

———. "Harold Pinter, Citizen." *The Pinter Review* (1989): 24–33.

———. "The Road to Basingstoke: *The Birthday Party* and the IRA." *The Pinter Review* (1993): 73–77.

Messenger, Anne P. "Blindness and the Problem of Identity in Pinter's Plays." *Die Neveren Sprachen* 8 (1972): 481–90.

Postlewaite, Thomas. "Pinter's *The Homecoming:* Displacing and Repeating Ibsen." *Comparative Drama* 15 (1981): 195–212.

Quigley, Austen. "*The Dumb Waiter:* Undermining the Tacit Dimension." *Modern Drama* 21, no. 1 (1978): 1–11.

Richardson, Brian. "Pinter's *Landscape* and the Boundaries of Narrative." *Essays in Literature* 18, no. 1 (1991): 37–45.

Schechner, R. "Puzzling Pinter." *Tulane Drama Review* 11, pt.2 (1966): 176–84.

Schiff, Ellen P. "Pancakes and Soap Suds: A Study of Childishness in Pinter's Plays." *Modern Drama* 16, no. 1 (1973): 91–101. An important topic dealt convincingly with here.

Smith, Leslie. "Pinter the Player." *Modern Drama* 22, no. 4 (1979): 349–63. Contains original research background material that illuminates *The Birthday Party,* particularly.

Suten, Anthony. " A Psycho-Aesthetic Approach to the Plays of Pinter." *Etudes Anglaises* 32 (1979): 414–24.

Thornton, Peter C. "Blindness and the Confrontation with Death." *Die Neveren Sprachen* 5 (1968): 213–33. One of several studies of blindness in Pinter. (See Messenger, "Blindness.")

Trilling, Ossia. "The New English Realism." *Tulane Drama Review* 7, pt.2 (1962): 184–93. The postwar context.

BIBLIOGRAPHY

Vannier, Jean. "A Theatre of Language." *Tulane Drama Review* 7, pt.3 (1963): 180–86. Though brief, a very important article concerned with Beckett, Adamov, and Ionesco, who, it is considered, have provided "a dramaturgy of human relations at the level of language itself." The applicability to Pinter's theater is extremely apposite.

Woodroffe, Grahame. "Taking Care of the 'Coloureds': The Political Metaphor of Harold Pinter's *The Caretaker.*" *Theatre Journal* 40 (1988): 498–508.

Interviews and Statements

The following selection includes significant examples that are reprinted or otherwise obtainable.

"A Letter to Peter Wood" (1958). Reprinted in Scott, *Harold Pinter.*

"Mr. Harold Pinter—Avant-Garde Playwright and Intimate Review." *The Times,* 16 November 1959, 4.

"Writing for Myself" (1961). *Plays Two.*

"Writing for the Theatre" (1962). *Plays One.*

"Harold Pinter: An Interview," with Lawrence Bensky (1972). Reprinted in Ganz, *Pinter: A Collection of Critical Essays.*

"In an Empty Bandstand—Harold Pinter in Conversation with Joan Bakewell." *The Listener* 82, no. 2119 (6 November 1969): 630–31.

"A Conversation [Pause] with Harold Pinter," with Mel Gussow (1990). *New York Times,* 5 December 1971. Reprinted in Gale, ed., *Critical Essays,* 15–33.

"Speech: Hamburg 1970." *Theatre Quarterly* 1 (1971): 3–4.

"A Play and Its Politics. A Conversation between Harold Pinter and Nicholas Hern" (1984); preface to *One for the Road,* 5–24.

"Radical Departures." *The Listener* 120, no. 3086 (27 October 1988): 4–6.

BIBLIOGRAPHY

"The 22 from Hackney to Chelsea: A Conversation with Harold Pinter."
Jewish Quarterly (Winter 1991–92): 9–17. With Barry Davis.

Gussow, Mel. *Conversations with Pinter*. London: Nicholas Hern Books,
1994.

Further Reading

Dobrez, L. A. C. *The Existential and Its Exits: Literary and Philosophical Perspectives in the Work of Beckett, Ionesco, Genet, and Pinter*.
London and New York: Athlone Press, St. Martin's Press, 1985. An
outstanding comparative study.

Dutton, Richard. *Modern Tragicomedy and the British Tradition:
Beckett, Pinter, Stoppard, Albee and Storey*. Brighton: Harvester
Press, 1986.

Esslin, Martin. *The Theatre of the Absurd*, rev. ed. Harmondsworth:
Penguin Books, 1968. Esslin's title applied a label to a major part of
avant-garde theater. In retrospect, it is perhaps less discriminating
than it at first appeared but is packed with information on every
page. Useful for reference.

Hewison, Robert. *In Anger: Culture in the Cold War, 1945–60*. London: Methuen, 1981. Good for social background.

Innes, Christopher. *Modern British Drama, 1890–1990*. Cambridge:
Cambridge University Press, 1992. The most informative and stimu-
lating survey available.

Kennedy, Andrew. *Six Dramatists in Search of a Language: Shaw, Eliot,
Beckett, Pinter, Osborne, Arden*. Cambridge: Cambridge University
Press, 1974. Excellent discussion of Pinter.

Newton, K. M. "Interpreting Pinter." *In Defence of Literary Interpretation: Theory and Practice*. London: Macmillan, 1986. Probably the
best single chapter available on the theoretical implications of critical approaches to Pinter.

BIBLIOGRAPHY

Nightingale, Benedict. *Fifty Modern British Plays*. London: Pan Books, 1982. In effect a very useful introduction.

Styan, J. L. *Modern Drama in Theory and Practice,* vol. 1: *Realism and Naturalism;* vol. 2: *Symbolism, Surrealism and the Absurd;* vol. 3: *Expressionism and Epic Theatre*. Cambridge: Cambridge University Press, 1981. Extremely valuable introductory handbooks, richly illustrated. Of basic utility in the study of any aspect of twentieth-century drama.

Taylor, John Russell. *Anger and After*. Harmondsworth: Penguin Books, 1963. Well-established contemporary study of the revolution in English drama from 1956.

In the last twenty years literary theory has developed in so many ramified ways that it is difficult for a newcomer to know where to start. The following two recent publications are outstanding works of reference.

Greenblatt, Stephen, and Giles Gunn, eds. *Redrawing the Boundaries: The Transformation of English and American Literary Studies*. New York: Modern Language Association of America, 1992.

Makaryk, Irena R, ed. *Encyclopedia of Contemporary Literary Theory*. Toronto: University of Toronto Press, 1993.

INDEX

INDEX

Dwarfs, The (fiction), 4, 72–73
Dwarfs, The, 33, 72–75, 77

Educating Rita, 95; *see also* Willy Russell
Eliot, T. S., 40, 42
Encore, 29
Epiphanies, 66, 128, 136–37, 156; *see also* Revue sketches
Esslin, Martin, 116
"Examination, The," 6, 63
Expressionism, 23, 33, 178, 202
Exton, Clive, 43

Family Voices, 147, 148–49, 205
Fascism, 2, 3, 29, 161, 170, 171, 173, 174–76, 191, 192, 197; *see also* Nazism
Feminism, 83, 94, 142
Film, 85; *see also* Samuel Beckett
Fitzgerald, F. Scott, 156–57
Flanagan, Bud, and Chesney Allen, 71
Flanagan, Pauline, 9
Foucault, Michel, 190
Fowles, John, 162
Fraser, Lady Antonia, 5
Fraser, J. G., 40
French Lieutenant's Woman, The, 5, 159, 162–64; *see also* John Fowles
Friel, Brian, 193
Friendship and betrayal, 18, 73, 74, 75, 77–78, 80, 86, 88, 89, 102–3, 138, 141–47, 172–74
Freud, Sigmund, 17, 35, 89, 107, 111, 116–18, 170

Galli-Curci, Amelia, 159
Galton, Alan, 30

INDEX

INDEX

INDEX

INDEX